Teen Pregnancy

by Jenny MacKay

LUCENT BOOKS

A part of Gale, Cengage Learning

GALE
CENGAGE Learning™

Detroit • New York • San Francisco • New Haven, Conn • Waterville, Maine • London

GALE
CENGAGE Learning™

LIBRARY OF CONGRESS CATALOGING-IN-PUBLICATION DATA

MacKay, Jenny, 1978-
  Teen pregnancy / by Jenny MacKay.
     p. cm. -- (Hot topics)
  Includes bibliographical references and index.
  ISBN 978-1-4205-0479-8 (hardcover)
  1. Teenage pregnancy. 2. Sex instruction for teenagers. 3. Birth control. 4. Abortion. I. Title.
  HQ759.4.M3325 2011
  306.874'3--dc22
                                                    2010053853

Lucent Books
27500 Drake Rd.
Farmington Hills, MI 48331

ISBN-13: 978-1-4205-0479-8
ISBN-10: 1-4205-0479-7

Printed in the United States of America
1 2 3 4 5 6 7 15 14 13 12 11

CONTENTS

FOREWORD

Young people today are bombarded with information. Aside from traditional sources such as newspapers, television, and the radio, they are inundated with a nearly continuous stream of data from electronic media. They send and receive e-mails and instant messages, read and write online "blogs," participate in chat rooms and forums, and surf the Web for hours. This trend is likely to continue. As Patricia Senn Breivik, the former dean of university libraries at Wayne State University in Detroit, has stated, "Information overload will only increase in the future. By 2020, for example, the available body of information is expected to double every 73 days! How will these students find the information they need in this coming tidal wave of information?"

Ironically, this overabundance of information can actually impede efforts to understand complex issues. Whether the topic is abortion, the death penalty, gay rights, or obesity, the deluge of fact and opinion that floods the print and electronic media is overwhelming. The news media report the results of polls and studies that contradict one another. Cable news shows, talk radio programs, and newspaper editorials promote narrow viewpoints and omit facts that challenge their own political biases. The World Wide Web is an electronic minefield where legitimate scholars compete with the postings of ordinary citizens who may or may not be well-informed or capable of reasoned argument. At times, strongly worded testimonials and opinion pieces both in print and electronic media are presented as factual accounts.

Conflicting quotes and statistics can confuse even the most diligent researchers. A good example of this is the question of whether or not the death penalty deters crime. For instance, one study found that murders decreased by nearly one-third when the death penalty was reinstated in New York in 1995. Death penalty supporters cite this finding to support their argument that the existence of the death penalty deters criminals from committing murder. However, another study found that states without the death penalty have murder rates below the national average. This study is cited by opponents of capital punishment, who reject the claim that the death penalty deters murder. Students need context and clear, informed discussion if they are to think critically and make informed decisions.

The Hot Topics series is designed to help young people wade through the glut of fact, opinion, and rhetoric so that they can think critically about controversial issues. Only by reading and thinking critically will they be able to formulate a viewpoint that is not simply the parroted views of others. Each volume of the series focuses on one of today's most pressing social issues and provides a balanced overview of the topic. Carefully crafted narrative, fully documented primary and secondary source quotes, informative sidebars, and study questions all provide excellent starting points for research and discussion. Full-color photographs and charts enhance all volumes in the series. With its many useful features, the Hot Topics series is a valuable resource for young people struggling to understand the pressing issues of the modern era.

THE BIRTH OF A SOCIAL DEBATE

Approximately 7 percent of all teenage girls in the United States become pregnant each year. Even though about four out of five pregnant teens are age eighteen or nineteen and are legally considered adults in American society, teenagers who are about to become parents are often referred to as kids having kids. Concerns are frequently raised about decisions and behaviors that lead to teen pregnancy and the ability of teenagers to handle the responsibility and consequences of childbearing at a young age. Pregnancy among teens is closely tied to religious and moral beliefs about marriage and families as well as arguments over whether young, unwed parents can create stable homes for their babies. There is also concern about the physical health and well-being of pregnant teens and their unborn children. Many pregnant and parenting teens face financial and social struggles, too, and they may create a social or economic burden on the rest of society.

The need to reduce the teen pregnancy rate and help pregnant teens make wise decisions about pregnancy has been an issue of public concern in the United States for decades. Nonetheless, there is little consensus about the best way to help America's teens avoid childbearing before they are ready. Abstinence and safe-sex initiatives are hotly debated. Americans also do not agree about how best to help teens cope with the situation if they do become pregnant and are facing the options of abortion, adoption, or keeping the baby. The varied opinions on these issues are often in the spotlight as the media frequently report on teen pregnancy, and recent high-profile teen pregnancies like those of Bristol Palin and Jamie Lynn Spears have drawn increased media attention to this controversial issue. Teen pregnancy has been a hot topic in social, health, educational, and political arenas in the United States for several generations, but public opinions about the issue remain widely varied.

Teen pregnancy has not always been so closely scrutinized. Before the 1960s it was usually taboo only if a young woman became pregnant before she was married. Pregnancy that did occur before marriage often resulted in a hastily planned wedding, even between teenagers. During the 1960s, however, American attitudes about sexual activity before marriage began to change. During a wave of support for feminism and women's rights, people started objecting to the double standard that caused women who had premarital sex to face more serious physical consequences and social prejudices than their male partners. The birth control pill also came on the market in the 1960s. This pill provides a dose of hormones that a woman can take daily to avoid an unplanned pregnancy. For the first time in history, women could now prevent childbearing by a means other than abstinence, and they began to think differently about sex. By the 1970s and 1980s, unmarried women and men of all ages, including teens, had launched a sexual revolution. The sexual practices of Americans changed as women, men, and teenagers felt freer to explore sexual relationships outside of marriage.

The occurrence of unplanned pregnancy, especially among teens, did not vanish with the invention of new birth control methods, however. In fact, the teen pregnancy rate in America began to climb steeply in the 1970s and 1980s, hitting the highest rates in recorded American history. This sparked public concern about the sexual morality of teenagers, the effectiveness of birth control medication, and the problem of children being born to women who were considered too young to raise them. It was also during this period—in 1973—that abortion was made legal in the United States.

Teen abortion rates began to climb along with the rate of teen pregnancy, setting off still more public concern that young women were using abortion as after-the-fact birth control, choosing to terminate their pregnancies instead of preventing them in the first place. By the late 1980s American society considered teen pregnancy one of the nation's most worrisome problems.

Approximately 7 percent of teenage girls in the United States get pregnant every year.

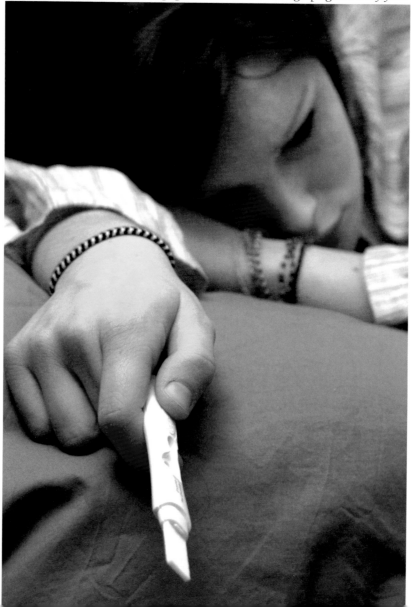

The teen pregnancy rate peaked in the United States in 1990. Then, for the next ten years, the annual number of teens who became pregnant began a steep and steady decline. The efforts of groups and agencies working to reduce teen pregnancy seemed successful. Yet during the early 2000s the decline leveled off, and in 2005 the teen pregnancy rate actually rose by 3 percent, causing renewed concern that nationwide strategies to reduce teen pregnancy had begun to fail. Even after a decade of progress, the United States still has a teen pregnancy rate higher than in any other country in the industrialized world. Teen pregnancy remains one of the major issues confronting American society today.

THE CAUSES OF TEEN PREGNANCY IN AMERICA

Nearly 750,000 young women age nineteen and younger become pregnant in the United States every year. Approximately one in three women gets pregnant before she reaches age twenty, according to the U.S. Centers for Disease Control and Prevention. This amounts to about seventy-two pregnancies out of every one thousand young women between the ages of fifteen and nineteen every year, and about seven pregnancies out of every one thousand teenage girls age fourteen or younger. Of these pregnancies, about 59 percent result in live births. Because the average age at the time of high school graduation is eighteen, many of these young women have not completed high school before they become mothers.

In modern American culture, a high school diploma is considered the minimum credential necessary to get a job that pays enough to provide for a family. According to the U.S. Census Bureau, 55 percent of American parents classified as poor have never completed high school, whereas only 24 percent of those not classified as poor lack a high school diploma. On the other hand, just 15 percent of parents in poor American families have any education past high school; 40 percent of parents who are not poor have pursued higher education. Children born to parents who have not completed high school are much more likely to be raised in a financially disadvantaged family.

Teen pregnancy is also a social issue, not just a financial one. The structure of family and the way children are raised are extremely important to human society. They determine how people live together in their communities and how social systems are built. Who bears children and who raises them are issues with wide-reaching consequences both for the current generation and for generations to come. Raising well-balanced, emotionally stable children who will become productive members of society requires a huge investment of time and resources, both from parents and from the community. Children born to teen parents who are not yet emotionally mature and prepared to raise them may suffer disadvantages that affect not only them as individuals but also the community to which they belong.

Because teen pregnancy trends have potentially negative effects on the future of American culture, both socially and financially, it is important to understand why many American teens are making choices that lead to pregnancy. Changing American values are often blamed. America's teen pregnancy rate has been compared with lesser rates in other countries, raising concerns that teens in the United States have become more promiscuous

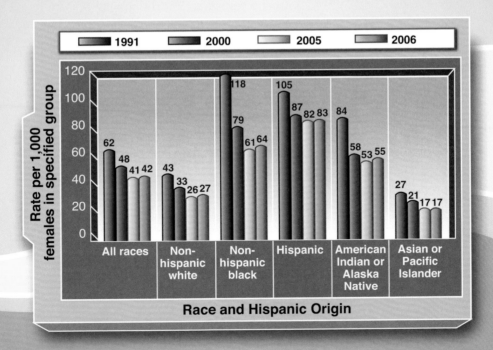

Teen Births by Race in the United States, 1991–2006

Taken from: CDC/NCHS. National Vital Statistics System. http://www.cdc.gov/nchs/data/factsheets/factsheet_nvss.htm.

and irresponsible than teens elsewhere. Yet there is also controversy over whether teenagers' moral values are truly in question or whether American society just is not tolerant or understanding of sexual relationships among teens, especially outside of marriage. Some of America's teens may also get pregnant in part because society portrays parenthood as such a positive life event for adults. These are some of the current viewpoints on the complex issue of teen pregnancy and its causes in America.

Are Teen Morals in Decline?

Many Americans who have conservative social views believe pregnancy among teens is a sign that America's morals have changed for the worse in the past several decades. The only way for teens to get pregnant is by having sex, something many conservative Americans believe is a much more common teen behavior now than it was fifty to sixty years ago and an indication that society's moral values, particularly sexual values, are in a state of decline. "Flip on the TV, peruse the Internet, or page through the average magazine on the newsstand today, and it is difficult to ignore the obvious: America's moral values seem to be slipping to new lows every year,"[1] says Dave Bohon, a journalist for the magazine *New American*. Some who claim that America's moral values are declining say teen pregnancy results from a society that has come to prize sexual freedom instead of sexual modesty and responsibility. "Sexually liberal elites have hijacked our culture," says Kerby Anderson, president of Probe Industries, Inc., a nonprofit corporation that focuses on preserving traditional values among Christians. Sexual liberalism, Anderson says, has "transformed the social landscape of America and made promiscuity a virtue and virginity a 'problem' to be solved."[2]

If American society truly is exposing teens to more sexual ideas at younger ages, it may also be pushing them to explore sexual activity earlier in life. Even teenagers comment on this trend. "It seems like our generation has matured sexually faster than generations previous to us,"[3] said a fourteen-year-old girl during an interview that aired on *Good Morning America* in 2008, and this sexual "maturity" is often flaunted when teens increasingly talk about and act on sexual impulses with little modesty

A High-Profile Pregnancy

In 2008 Alaska governor Sarah Palin was running for vice president of the United States and taking a conservative stance on issues such as taxes and family values. During her election campaign, the Republican candidate and mother of five learned that one of her daughters, seventeen-year-old Bristol Palin, was pregnant. News of the pregnancy brought many notoriously divisive issues between Democrats and Republicans to the forefront, including the debates over abstinence education, unwed pregnancy, and abortion. The media and the nation were intensely interested in Bristol's decisions throughout the presidential campaign. Some Democrats claimed that having a pregnant teenage daughter belied Sarah Palin's commitment to family values and proved that Republican-supported abstinence education was an obvious failure. Many Republicans, meanwhile, commended Bristol's pregnancy because she had not chosen to have an abortion and had instead committed herself to raising her child and accepting responsibility for her actions. Although Bristol was only one among hundreds of thousands of pregnant teenagers that year, her pregnancy became uniquely famous and brought to light the highly political issue that teen pregnancy in the United States has become. Bristol, now a mother, has worked as an advocate to help teenagers in America make choices to avoid becoming pregnant before they are ready.

The pregnancy of Sarah Palin's daughter, Bristol, (second from right) brought debates over abstinence education, unwed pregnancy, and abortion to the forefront of the 2008 presidential campaign.

or consideration of the consequences. Some Americans believe that casual, meaningless sex has become a common behavior for teens in America, and there is concern that today's teens may care more about their immediate moods and feelings than about their future, education, and moral values. Teen pregnancy is one potentially negative consequence of impulsive teen behavior. Among those concerned about the possible outcomes of all this teen sexuality—outcomes such as teen pregnancy—are many teenagers themselves. "Kids should not be worrying about 'I have to get diapers for my baby,' when I'm 16, 17 years old,"[4] a fifteen-year-old boy told *Good Morning America*.

Have Teen Morals Really Changed?

Not all Americans agree that American society is losing its moral values, however, or that sexual activity among teens is any more common now than in decades past. In fact, teenage birth rates have actually declined overall since the 1950s. "The teen birth rate has continued to fall steadily," say teen pregnancy researchers Saul D. Hoffman and Rebecca A. Maynard, and despite a slight increase in 2005, the rate is still "about 33 percent below its 1991 peak."[5] Citing numbers from a teen pregnancy study performed by the Guttmacher Institute, an organization that researches sexual and reproductive health worldwide, Hoffman and Maynard say that even though a long decline in the pregnancy rate among American teens ages fifteen to nineteen leveled off between 2005 and 2006, that year nevertheless marked "the lowest rate ever recorded for U.S. teens in the 65 years for which consistent data are available."[6]

Statistics like these undermine claims that American teenagers are more sexually active now than in the past. According to sociologist and criminal justice professor Kathleen A. Bogle, the public's alarm over teen sexuality and its ties to pregnancy rates may be uncalled for, at least for older teens. "The virginity rate in college is higher than you think and the number of [sexual] partners is lower than you think," she says. "But so many people think we're morally in trouble, in a downward spiral and teens are out of control. It's very difficult to convince people otherwise."[7] The overall downward trend in the teen pregnancy rate

Recent statistics compiled by the Guttmacher Institute undermine the claim that teenagers are more sexually active than in the past.

in America since the 1980s indicates that the United States may not be facing a growing moral crisis of teenage sexuality after all.

Are U.S. Teens More Promiscuous than Others?

Even though the pregnancy rate among teenagers has reached historic lows within the United States in the past decade, American teens are nevertheless far more likely to get pregnant than are teenage girls in most other Western industrialized nations that have a similar standard of living to that of the United States. The rate of pregnancy among U.S. teenagers is about twice the rate in Great Britain and Canada and about four times the rate in Sweden and France. It is also about twice as high as Australia's teen pregnancy rate, seven times as high as Italy's, and eight times as high as Japan's. The high proportion of pregnancies that occur among American teens every year compared with most other countries with similarly advanced economies and standards of living could suggest that American children are learning about sex not only too early but also in the wrong ways. According to the Family Connection of St. Joseph County, a nonprofit child and family research organization in Indiana, "The American culture glorifies sex and ignores responsibility. Beginning in early childhood, young people are bombarded with sexual messages. At the same time, puritanical attitudes restrict the availability of resources and frank discussions about sex."[8] This has led to the suggestion that American society may differ from other countries by encouraging sexuality among teenagers without preparing them adequately for the possible consequences of sex, such as pregnancy.

A DRASTIC SITUATION

"Out-of-wedlock teen birth is driving every single rotten outcome in our city."—Krista Ruth, former social policy adviser for Indianapolis, Indiana.

Quoted in Wanda S. Pillow, *Unfit Subjects: Educational Policy and the Teen Mother.* New York: RoutledgeFalmer, 2004, p. 17.

Teenagers in the United States are having sex earlier in life than their peers in other developed countries, too, according to statistics on the number of sexually active American teenagers and the age at which they lost their virginity. The Guttmacher Institute reports that about 70 percent of American teenagers have had sex at least once by the time

Studies indicate that British and European teens become sexually active about a year later than American teenagers do.

A Pact to Get Pregnant

In June 2008 news of seventeen pregnant students at Gloucester High School in Gloucester, Massachusetts, hit national headlines. The number of teen pregnancies at the school that year was four times the school's average annual pregnancy rate, four pregnancies per its twelve hundred students. More shocking was the news that the pregnancies were the result of a pact among a group of girls who decided to deliberately get pregnant and then raise their babies together. The story, first reported in *Time* magazine, described a large number of girls going to the school's health clinic for pregnancy tests during the school year and giving each other high fives if the tests were positive or seeming disappointed if not. The pregnant girls denied that there had ever been a pact, saying instead that a few girls, upon learning they were pregnant, had promised to support one another through their pregnancies. No formal proof of a pregnancy pact was ever uncovered. The pact itself may have been a mere rumor, but it spread around the world and was reported as far away as Australia and Brazil, highlighting on a global scale America's intense controversy over teen pregnancy.

Carolyn Kirk, mayor of Gloucester, Massachusetts, talks to members of the press about the alleged pregnancy pact at a local school. No formal proof of the pact was ever uncovered.

they are nineteen, and the average age at which teenagers become sexually active in the United States is seventeen—about a year younger than sexually active teens in Sweden, France, Canada, and Great Britain. Not only are American teens sexually active at earlier ages than teens in many other developed countries, they also tend to have more sexual partners. According to the Guttmacher Institute, "American teenagers who had intercourse in the past year are more likely to have had more than one partner than young people in the other countries, especially those in France and Canada."[9]

The fact that so many more teenage pregnancies occur in the United States than in other developed countries every year could imply that American culture does not adequately educate teens about sex and its possible outcomes, especially pregnancy. "Contributors [to the rise in teen pregnancy] include an over-sexualized culture, lack of involved and positive role models, and the dominant message that teen sex is expected and without consequences,"[10] says Valerie Huber of the National Abstinence Education Association. When America's high teen pregnancy rate is compared with that of other countries, loose morals again receive much of the blame. "Asked to identify the most serious problem confronting youth, American adults answered that it is the failure of adolescents to learn moral values,"[11] say child psychologists Daniel Hart and Gustavo Carlo. Some people believe that if American society adopted more restrictive values and beliefs about sex, marriage, and family, teen sexuality and teen pregnancy rates would drop closer to the rates of other developed countries. Nevertheless, even though U.S. teenagers begin having sex at younger ages and have higher pregnancy rates than teens in other similarly developed countries around the world, many young people in those countries do become sexually active while still in their teens. In fact, research by the Guttmacher Institute shows that by the time they are nineteen years old, just as many teens are sexually active in other countries as in the United States. According to social health experts Andrew L. Cherry, Mary E. Dillon, and Douglas Rugh, it is not true that teenagers in America have more interest in sex than do teenagers in other countries. "In most of the world, the majority of young women become sexually active during their teenage years," they say. "A majority of women and men become sexually active by age 20—in developed and developing countries alike."[12] What differs most between the United States and countries with lower teen pregnancy rates is not necessarily teen interest in sex but the public's perception that teen sexuality is morally wrong. "Countries other than the United States have attitudes more accepting of adolescent sexual behavior,"[13] the Guttmacher Institute reports. Adult Americans, in contrast, tend to look down on teen sex.

Premarital Sex Could Be the Real Controversy

American adults who disapprove of teenage sex may see it as irresponsible behavior that has caused the rates of teen pregnancy in the United States to soar in the past few decades. However, just as there is little difference in the sexuality of nineteen-year-olds across international borders, there has also been little change in the sexuality of American teens since the 1950s. Contrary to widely held beliefs about uncontrolled teen sex in modern America, the teen pregnancy rate in the United States is not higher than it was generations ago. In fact, American teenagers are actually less likely to have babies now than in previous decades, suggesting that teens were at least as sexually active back then as are modern teens. "It may come as a surprise to learn that the teen birth rate was 50% higher in 1957 than it is now,"[14] says the Family Connection of St. Joseph County. Yet during the 1950s teen pregnancy did not raise concerns over society's values, and the sexual activity of American teens was not routinely compared with that of other countries in those days either. The Family Connection explains a possible reason for the change: "Today's widespread concern over teen pregnancy may have less to do with actual numbers and more to do with the growing numbers of teen mothers who are unmarried."[15] Author and public speaker Frederica Mathewes-Green agrees. "Teen pregnancy is not the problem," she says. "'Unwed' teen pregnancy is the problem. It's childbearing outside marriage that causes all the trouble."[16]

The average age of marriage in the United States is twenty-five for women and twenty-seven for men. This average is several years higher than it was in the 1950s, when teenagers who were pregnant before age twenty were far more likely to be married than are pregnant teens in America today. Although the age of marriage has risen significantly in the past few decades, many Americans' ideas about family values and sexual morals have changed little. The result is that many teens are having sex, as they have throughout history and as they do almost everywhere around the world, but most of American society still believes that pregnancy ideally should be put off until marriage. Since most pregnant teens are not getting married, there is a widespread opinion that they should not be having sex either.

NOT THE END OF THE WORLD

"Most teens do not want to become parents and are not ready to take on the responsibilities of raising children. Nonetheless, teenage parenthood is simply not the disastrous and life-compromising event that it has been portrayed to be."—Frank F. Furstenberg, chair of the MacArthur Foundation Research Network on Transitions to Adulthood.

Frank F. Furstenberg, *Destinies of the Disadvantaged: The Politics of Teenage Childbearing.* New York: Russell Sage Foundation, 2007, p. 10.

In contrast, European countries tend to have more open attitudes about teen sexuality and sex outside of marriage. This disparity in attitudes toward teen sexuality can be seen in European sexual education programs. "Pragmatic, straightforward sexuality education has reduced teen pregnancy . . . in Western Europe," say Cherry, Dillon, and Rugh. "Due in part to public and political resistance to such measures, the United States lags behind other developed countries in the extent to which teenage fertility has declined."[17]

In the four developed countries with which the Guttmacher Institute compared the United States in the early 2000s, there is general acceptance of teen sexuality as long as it happens within a committed, mature relationship. In the United States, by contrast, teens are more likely to get the message that teenage sex is wrong altogether because they are still too young to be married. "While adults in the other study countries focus chiefly on the quality of young people's relationships and the exercise of personal responsibility within those relationships," says the Guttmacher Institute, "adults in the United States are often more concerned about whether young people are having sex. Close relationships are viewed as worrisome because they may lead to intercourse."[18]

Teens in Western countries with lower teen pregnancy rates than in the United States tend to receive more information about and support for birth control and safe-sex practices than American teens. In the United States teenagers are often advised to avoid sex completely, and information about and access to birth control are not always consistent or easy to find. "What a humiliating contrast to Europe and Canada, whose teens have intercourse at roughly the same rate as Americans, but whose national policies on sex education and health have been dramatically more successful in curtailing pregnancy,"[19] says marriage, family, and sex therapist Marty Klein. In Europe, says Susie Wilson, founder of a teen sexuality website called Sex, Etc., "their whole society says: 'We're going to teach you . . . we're not going to punish you.' If you talked to European teens, they have a much more healthy aspect about sex."[20] The high teen pregnancy rate in the United States may result not from poor values and morals but from a society that fails to accept and support its sexually active—and usually unmarried—teenagers.

Teen Pregnancy Is Not Necessarily Bad

Yet another possible explanation for the high rate of teen pregnancy in the United States versus similarly developed countries is that American society's values are perhaps more child-friendly altogether. Society should not assume that all teenage pregnancies are accidental and unwanted. According to the Guttmacher Institute, "Teenage women in the United States are more likely than their peers in other countries to want to become mothers."[21] The CDC reports that about one in five sexually active teenage girls and one in four sexually active teenage boys in the United States say they would be pleased about a pregnancy. Even if the only U.S. teenagers who became pregnant were

Teenage women in the United States are more likely than their peers in other countries to want to become pregnant.

those who wanted to, the Guttmacher Institute says, the number of pregnancies among teens in the United States would still be higher than the total number, wanted or unwanted, in France and Sweden and about two-thirds as high as the total number in Great Britain and Canada.

These statistics could mean that American culture is simply fonder of pregnancy and babies than are cultures in other countries. Overall, having babies is typically considered a very positive life event in America. "Americans are just generally more optimistic and child-friendly than many countries,"[22] says Nancy Gibbs, a reporter for *Time* magazine. "Americans like children," agrees Nan Marie Astone, a professor of population, family, and reproductive health. "We are the only people who respond to prosperity by saying, 'let's have another kid.'"[23] It is possible that some teenagers who become pregnant are caught up in America's love of babies and children. The high teen pregnancy rate in the United States might ultimately reflect a culture that prizes children and family, not a culture where family values are in decline.

The teen pregnancy rate does not necessarily reflect a culture of impulsive and irresponsible teenagers either. "We're convinced that young people are simply incapable of adult responsibility," says Mathewes-Green. "We expect that they will have poor control of their impulses, be self-centered and emotional, and be incapable of visualizing consequences." She says these low expectations of teenagers are a fairly recent development. "It wasn't always that way; through much of history, teen marriage and childbearing was the norm."[24] American society may give too little credit to its teenagers and their ability to behave as responsible adults. These low expectations might contribute to the perception that teenagers are incapable of coping maturely with sexual relationships and their consequences. Thus, teen pregnancy may be perceived as a bigger problem than it would be if society generally believed teens could be mature and responsible parents.

The Controversy Continues

Despite strong and differing opinions about teen pregnancy, its causes, and what it means for modern American society, it is a situation Americans must continue to study. Teen pregnancy sparks much debate in many areas of society, including public health and public education. Responding to the issue will likely require a widespread and unbiased approach. The Family Connection of St. Joseph County says, "If we are truly concerned about the welfare of babies, children and adolescents, we must move beyond the moral panic and denial that so often distort the [teen pregnancy] discussion."[25] Although highly controversial, teen pregnancy is not something that Americans can readily ignore. "Every culture has to deal with the sexuality of its young people,"[26] Klein says.

Is Teen Pregnancy a Public Health Problem?

In addition to its role in discussions of society's morals, teen pregnancy is often referred to as a public health problem, which is a health issue with a negative effect on communities, the nation, or even the world. Because of their widespread nature and their negative consequences, public health problems are important concerns for society to address. Whereas doctors, nurses, and other health care professionals concentrate on treating one patient at a time, public health professionals concentrate on identifying which health issues are the most common, the most dangerous, and the most costly across an entire society and try to find solutions to reduce the harmful effects of those health issues. To be classified as a public health problem, a disease or health condition must occur or have the potential to occur among many people. It must pose significant risks to people's personal health, safety, productivity, and well-being, and it also must create a significant cost or tragedy burden on individual patients, on hospitals, and on society as a whole.

Once a condition or illness is classified as a public health issue, health officials work to find reasonable methods for responding to the problem and reducing its effects. The methods of treating or reacting to the problem generally must be acceptable both to patients and to society. Yet because it usually takes a lot of money and resources to address public health problems, and because laws and other changes to public policy are often a result, the decision of whether a particular health issue actually qualifies as a public health problem is usually a controversial one. For decades people have been debating whether teen pregnancy meets the criteria, and if so, what the public's response to this health problem should be.

The Health Risks to Pregnant Teenagers

Common health risks and dangers of pregnancy can be more serious for a teenager than for an adult woman due to the teenager's younger age and the fact that she still may be developing

Pregnant teenagers are about 35 percent less likely than adult women to seek prenatal care.

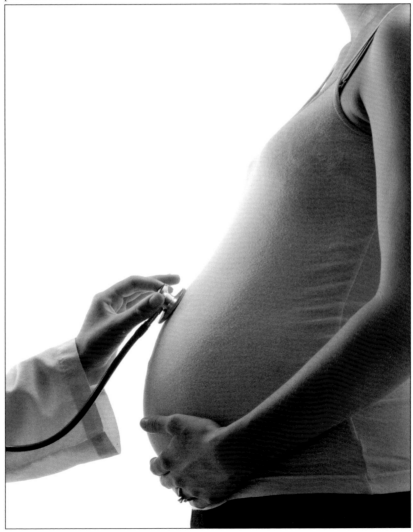

physically. Adolescents have a higher risk of certain pregnancy-related health problems than adult women do. The bodies of teenagers, especially those younger than age sixteen, may not be physically mature and prepared for the pregnancy process. Due to greater possible threats to their health, pregnant teenagers benefit from a doctor's guidance throughout their pregnancy. "Adolescents, because of increased maternal and fetal risks, require special prenatal management," says Joanne E. Cox, a professor of pediatrics at Harvard Medical School. "Prenatal care is a major factor predicting a positive outcome for a teen birth."[27] The Centers for Disease Control and Prevention (CDC), however, reports that pregnant teenagers are about 35 percent less likely than adult women to seek health care regularly from the start of their pregnancy. According to the Guttmacher Institute, about 7 percent of pregnant teenagers in the United States receive little or no health care during pregnancy. This may be because they are ashamed and do not want anyone to know about the pregnancy, they do not have the money to pay for doctor visits, they have no way to get to the doctor's office, or they are unaware of the importance of regular prenatal care. Whatever their reasons, many pregnant teens are reluctant to seek the medical treatment that can help them minimize or manage the possible health risks of pregnancy. This leads some people to consider teen pregnancy a public health problem with potentially serious consequences for teenage girls and their unborn babies.

One major health risk for pregnant teenagers is malnutrition. A teenage girl's body may still be maturing, especially if she is younger than sixteen. If she becomes pregnant, some of the nutrients her body needs for its own development may be shifted to her baby instead, leaving her undernourished and possibly unhealthy. Not all pregnant teenagers become malnourished. Those who eat a balanced diet, gain the amount of weight that is healthy for a pregnant woman, and take recommended nutrition supplements are very likely to stay nutritionally healthy during and after pregnancy. Yet for teens accustomed to unhealthy diets, poor nutrition often continues into pregnancy. If pregnant teens do not seek health care early in their pregnancies, they may remain unaware of the importance of good nutrition for the health of themselves and their babies. Others, wanting to avoid weight gain during pregnancy or not wanting their pregnancy to be obvious to anyone, may even try to diet so they stay slim. "Because body image is extremely important to the adolescent, she may use behaviors associated with eating disorders, such as purging [forced vomiting after meals] or self-starvation, to avoid weight gain during the pregnancy,"[28] says pediatric nursing specialist Nancy T. Hatfield. In the process, these teens could be denying themselves important nutrients and risking nutrition problems such as anemia, which is an iron deficiency that is common during pregnancy and often leads to exhaustion, shortness of breath, and other problems.

PREGNANCY AS AN ESCAPE

"Pregnancy [is] sometimes viewed as a means of escape: escape from having to go to school, from the community, or from an unhappy home."—Linda Archibald, teen pregnancy researcher and policy consultant.

Linda Archibald, "Teenage Pregnancy in Inuit Communities: Issues and Perspectives," Pauktuutit Inuit Women's Association, April 2004. www.pauktuutit.ca/pdf/publications/pauktuutit/teenpregnancy_e.pdf.

Pregnant teenagers are also at greater risk than women in their twenties and thirties of developing preeclampsia. Preeclampsia is a condition that causes dangerously high blood pressure during pregnancy and can result in swelling of the hands, legs, and feet. If it is not treated, a severe case can cause seizures, a coma, and possibly even death of the mother, her unborn child, or both. Preeclampsia can occur in any pregnant woman, but it is most common among teenagers and women older than age forty, especially if it is a woman's first pregnancy. Preeclampsia usually can be controlled with proper medical care, but pregnant teenagers who do not get regular checkups during pregnancy may be unaware of the signs and symptoms of preeclampsia; therefore, they may be at greater risk for serious problems if they develop it.

Another pregnancy-related health problem that tends to be worse among pregnant teens is depression. This serious medi-

Pregnant teenagers tend to be more depressed than adult women and this can lead to serious health issues.

cal condition is marked by severe, constant, long-lasting, and overwhelming feelings of sadness and hopelessness. Women of any age can experience depression during or soon after pregnancy, often because pregnancy-related hormone changes affect their moods. Depression is also common among teenagers in general, a result of hormone changes and emotional struggles during puberty and adolescence. For teens who become pregnant, the combination of age and pregnancy makes depression especially common and often very severe. "The prevalence of depression among pregnant adolescents . . . is almost twice as high as among adult pregnant women and nonpregnant adolescents,"[29] say psychiatrists Eva M. Szigethy and Pedro Ruiz. Depression is a serious health problem that can have major effects on a person's quality of life and motivation to do things like work or study. It can even lead to attempts at self-harm or suicide, making it a potentially life-threatening complication of pregnancy. The increased risk of depression in pregnant adolescents is another reason why teen pregnancy could be considered a public health problem.

Risky Births

Pregnant teens who give birth to their babies also may be at greater risk of serious injury and even death during childbirth than physically mature women in their twenties and thirties. Giving birth can be dangerous for any woman, regardless of her age. The birth process sometimes results in such emergencies as hemorrhaging (extremely heavy and often fatal bleeding), a breech birth (in which the fetus is turned in such a way that it cannot pass through the birth canal), or a life-threatening infection. Overall, death during childbirth is very rare in the United States, where only about eight women in every hundred thousand who give birth do not survive, according to the CDC. However, pregnant girls ages seventeen and younger are twice as likely to die while giving birth than are mothers who are older than seventeen, says pediatrician Jonathan D. Klein, adding that "these risks may be greatest for the youngest teenagers."[30] Around the world, when developing and underdeveloped countries are taken into account, childbirth is actually the leading cause of death among girls ages fifteen to nineteen. This statistic suggests that pregnancy itself poses a real danger to teenagers. "The health risks of teenage pregnancy are very high," writes Stephen Maddocks of the United Nations Children's Fund, an international organization that supports education and health programs for children around the world. "In many cases," he states, "the girl's body is not yet ready to give birth."[31]

Health Problems in Unborn Children

The possible health risks that a teenage mother faces during pregnancy are only half of the problem. A pregnancy involves at least one other person—the unborn baby or, in cases of twins or other multiples, babies. Pregnancy during the teenage years not only puts added strain on a young woman's body but also often results in health problems for the unborn child. These health issues more commonly arise in teen pregnancies. One of the most widespread and potentially harmful problems is preterm labor and delivery, which happens when the mother goes into labor too early (three weeks or more before the end of the forty-week term that is the standard length of a normal pregnancy). Babies born before the thirty-seventh week of pregnancy are called premature, and they are more likely to have various health problems than babies who are born at or near the end of the pregnancy term. These problems include brain damage and difficulty with breathing and digesting. About 9 percent of all babies born in America are premature, but among teenage mothers, the premature birthrate is higher—about 15 percent. The health effects of being born too early are so serious that many experts see premature birth itself as an issue of public health. "Prematurity, birth before 37 completed weeks' gestation, is one of the greatest public health problems in the United States today," says Barbara Luke, a professor of public health. "Premature babies— preemies—are more than merely small. They are developmentally unprepared for life outside the uterus. . . . For example, children who were born premature are more likely to have respiratory problems during childhood, as well as a higher

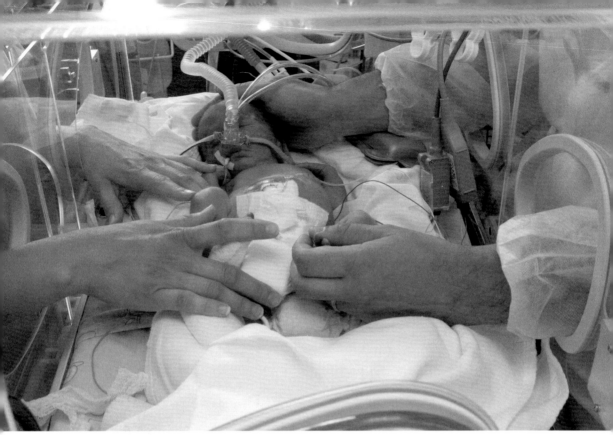

Fifteen percent of teen births are premature. Premature birth can lead to childhood respiratory problems and increase the incidences of learning disabilities, speech, hearing, and vision problems later in life.

incidence of learning disabilities and problems with speech, hearing, and vision"[32] later in life.

Another potentially serious problem that commonly affects babies born to teen mothers is low birth weight. Babies who weigh 5.5 pounds (2.5kg) or less at birth have a high risk for many health problems during infancy and even into childhood and adult life. As infants, low-birth-weight babies are at greater risk for problems such as asthma and other breathing difficulties as well as heart and brain defects that occur because their small bodies had not developed fully before birth. When they grow into adults, low-birth-weight babies have as much as a tenfold higher risk of developing high blood pressure, diabetes, and heart disease. Premature babies are more likely to have a low birth weight than babies born after at least thirty-seven weeks of pregnancy, but about one in ten pregnant teenagers who give birth have a baby with a low birth weight, even if the baby is

The Cost of Teen Pregnancy

Pregnancy and childbirth among unmarried teenagers cost the U.S. government billions of dollars in welfare every year. In an effort to keep these costs under control, the government created the Temporary Assistance for Needy Families (TANF) program in 1996 to replace what had previously been an open-ended welfare program with few limits on the length of time needy parents could receive benefits. Under TANF, each state receives a certain amount of money from the federal government that it can use to help families with children. In order to receive TANF funds, states must create programs to reduce births to unmarried mothers, encourage the formation of two-parent families, and promote education and job preparation among parents who receive TANF money. An adult can accept help from TANF for a maximum of five years during his or her lifetime, which the program's supporters believe will eliminate lifelong dependency on welfare and make recipients more self-sufficient. Critics of TANF argue that five years may not be long enough, especially for recipients who become parents as teenagers. Despite many controversies over TANF, it is one of the major sources of welfare funding for teenage parents in the United States.

not born prematurely. The younger a teenage mother is during her pregnancy, the more likely she is to give birth to a low-birth-weight baby. This may occur either because her own body is still developing and competing with the baby for important nutrients or because she did not take good care of herself during pregnancy. "What female adolescents do to and with their bodies is a causative factor in the higher incidence of low birth weight babies," say adolescent health instructors Jeffrey Roth, Jo Hendrickson, Max Schilling, and Daniel W. Stowell. "Some pregnant teens resist medical advice . . . concerned with their body image and testing social boundaries, some teens fail to eat properly."[33] Because of the high incidence of low-birth-weight babies among teens—and the serious and costly health problems that persist as these children grow into adulthood—many observers believe that teen pregnancy should be classified as a public health problem.

Disabled Babies

Babies born to teenage mothers also have a higher risk of being born with certain disabilities that are caused by nutrition deficits in a mother's body early in pregnancy. One example is neural tube defects, which are imperfections in the baby's brain and spinal cord. These areas begin to develop very early in a pregnancy, often before the mother is even aware that she is pregnant. A common neural tube defect is spina bifida, a condition in which the baby's spine does not develop fully, usually causing the baby to be paralyzed at birth. Neural tube defects like spina bifida have been linked to a deficiency in folic acid—a B vitamin essential to a baby's spine and brain development—in the mother's body during the first few weeks of pregnancy. Neural tube defects are irreversible and can cause lifelong disability and health issues after birth. According to the University of Rochester Medical Center in New York, babies born to teenage mothers are more likely to be born with spina bifida than babies born to adult women, perhaps because most teens are not expecting to get pregnant and do not realize that they need to take folic acid supplements before and during pregnancy. Although spina bifida is a rare condition, occurring in only one out of every thousand babies, it is an important example of how teen pregnancy poses certain serious health risks to unborn babies that are not as common in children born to older mothers.

Why Teen Pregnancy Is a Public Health Problem

Health risks that are more serious or more common among pregnant teenagers and their babies than in pregnancies among women who are older bolster the argument that teen pregnancy should be classified as a public health problem in the United States. Teen pregnancy meets the major criteria of a public health problem: It is widespread, occurring among hundreds of thousands of teens and their infants each year, and it affects the health, safety, well-being, and productivity of many teens and their infants in negative ways. The health risks of being pregnant at a young age are also costly to society, putting a potential burden on the doctors and hospitals that treat pregnant teens and provide continued care for newborn children

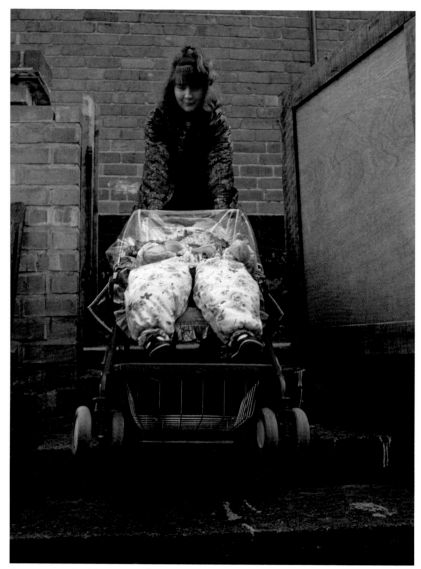

Approximately 80 percent of teenage mothers turn to government welfare to help provide basic needs.

who have chronic health conditions such as those due to being born prematurely. Because many teens have not finished high school before they have a child, they are less likely than high school graduates to have a job that pays enough to support a family. According to the Child Trends DataBank, about 80 percent of teenage mothers end up relying on welfare, money the government gives to low-income citizens to help provide for their needs. For some pregnant teenagers, both during pregnancy and after the birth, these needs include costly medical expenses, supporting the argument that teen pregnancy is an issue with negative effects not only on individual patients but on society as a whole. "The personal and society impact of teenage pregnancy in the United States is huge," says nursing professor Nweze Eunice Nnakwe. "Teenage pregnancy is a major public health problem."[34]

Hard to Say No

"There are cultural norms and pressures in this society that make it hard for teens to just say no [to sex], particularly if they lack opportunities to say yes to something else."—Deborah Rhode, Stanford University law professor.

Quoted in Stanford University News Service, "Teen Pregnancy: Economics More Important than Age," September 20, 1993. www.stanford.edu/dept/news/pr/93/931020Arc3093.html.

There are ways American society might be able to reduce or prevent the health risks associated with teen pregnancy, which is another important criterion of public health problems. Though, says Kathleen Sylvester, vice president of a national research and education organization called the Progressive Policy Institute, "it has been more convenient to declare preventing teen pregnancy 'beyond the capacity of government' than to take an unequivocal moral position against it and take steps to reverse the trend." Sylvester says more can and should be done to address teen pregnancy as a preventable public health problem: "We must acknowledge our urgent and compelling national interest in preventing pregnancies by young women unprepared to be mothers."[35] Just as there are public campaigns such as "Stamp Out Smoking" to teach people about the health-related dangers of cigarettes, public policies could also be developed to educate teenagers about the health risks of pregnancy before age twenty. "Progress in reducing teen pregnancy and childbearing will not only improve the well-being of children, families, and communities, but will also reduce the burden on taxpayers,"[36] says the National Campaign to Prevent Teen and Unplanned Pregnancy, an organization whose goal is to reduce unplanned pregnancies in America, especially among teens. Classifying teen pregnancy as a public health problem might give these organizations and others like them the public support they require in their efforts to address teen pregnancy.

Why Teen Pregnancy Is Not a Public Health Problem

Pregnancy among teenagers is associated with added health risks to the mothers and their children, but some Americans argue that the true impact of teen pregnancy on the health of society may be overestimated. Although pregnant teenagers do have a higher risk for some pregnancy-related health problems, especially if they are younger than sixteen, the majority of teen pregnancies (about 80 percent) in the United States occur among teens who are eighteen or nineteen years old. Women in this older teenage group actually have a lower rate of health problems overall—and, in fact, may even be healthier during pregnancy—than other age groups, particularly women older than age thirty-five. For example, when compared with mothers older than thirty-five, pregnant teens have about half the risk of requiring a costly emergency procedure called a cesarean section, in which the baby is surgically removed from the uterus during birth. Pregnant women who are thirty-five or older also have about fourteen times the risk of giving birth to a baby with a lifelong disabling condition called Down syndrome, caused by a genetic abnormality, than mothers who are teenagers. And pregnant women older than thirty-five have similar (and often even higher) risks as teenagers of pregnancy complications such as preeclampsia, giving birth prematurely, and having a baby with a low birth weight. "So where is the public health crisis?" says Janet Rich-Edwards of the Harvard

Newborns Murdered

In 1997 a New Jersey high school student gave birth in the bathroom during her senior prom, disposed of her infant in the bathroom garbage can, and then went back to the dance. Such stories of neonaticide—the killing of a newborn within the first few hours of life—horrify the public. Because those who commit this crime are usually unwed teenagers or women in their early twenties, neonaticide has been used to portray pregnant teens as potentially cruel and unfit for parenthood. Yet studies have shown that young women who commit neonaticide are rarely criminally minded. Instead, most are traumatized about pregnancy to the extent that they may be in denial of it. "For many women,

pregnancy raises fears of interpersonal abandonment," says psychiatrist Laura J. Miller. "For example, some adolescents who denied their pregnancies had been told they would be kicked out of the house if they became pregnant." When she gives birth, usually all alone, a teen who is in denial may panic at the reality of the baby and harm or abandon it without thinking of consequences. Neonaticide accounts for only about 2 to 3 percent of all homicides, but it highlights many controversial issues about teen pregnancy, its contributing factors, and its sometimes drastic consequences.

Quoted in Margaret G. Spinelli, ed., *Infanticide: Psychosocial and Legal Perspectives on Mothers Who Kill.* Washington, DC: American Psychiactric, 2003, p. 11.

Melissa Drexler was indicted for murdering her newborn son at her senior prom.

Medical School. "If there is a real health cost of teen pregnancy, we are hard put to measure it."[37]

Teen pregnancy is often debated as a public health problem, but pregnancy over age thirty-five, which carries at least as many health risks, is not. People's concern over the "problem" of teen pregnancy may have more to do with the economic and social position of teens in society than with the actual health risks of teen pregnancy. "There are no inherent health or medical problems associated with becoming pregnant and having a child before the age of twenty," say Debbie A. Lawlor and Mary Shaw of the Department of Social Medicine at the University of Bristol in the United Kingdom. "If society were such that a 16-year-old could begin her family at that age, and then say in her mid-twenties, return to education or a chosen career path, without prejudice and undue uphill struggle, there would be no problem."[38]

Teen pregnancy and any associated health complications also might not be as widespread as they seem at first glance. Although approximately 750,000 girls and young women under age twenty get pregnant each year, only about 59 percent of them complete their pregnancy, according to the Guttmacher Institute. About 27 percent of pregnant teens choose to have an abortion, and another 14 percent of teen pregnancies end in miscarriage (when a pregnancy is terminated due to natural causes). Less than half a million (about 443,000) pregnant teenagers in the United States actually complete their pregnancy and are therefore at risk of health complications related to full-term pregnancy and birth. Compared with widespread health problems such as cancer (affecting 11 million Americans), diabetes (affecting 24 million Americans), or heart disease (affecting 81 million Americans), many experts do not consider teen pregnancy and its health risks to constitute a major public health issue. "The scale of teenage pregnancy and childbearing is often overestimated,"[39] says children's public health researcher Lisa Arai.

Calling teen pregnancy a health problem, some researchers say, might generate undue public concern and could actually make the situation worse. "We do not believe that labeling a woman who chooses to have a baby under the age of twenty as a public health problem actually helps the mother or her child," say Lawlor and Shaw. "We believe that the underlying problem lies in society's attitudes towards young people and specifically in attitudes towards women's reproductive lives."[40] Classifying teen pregnancy as a public health problem implies that pregnant teenagers and their babies will have health problems and that becoming pregnant as a teenager is an unhealthy event,

In the United States 59 percent of women under age twenty complete their pregnancy while 27 percent have an abortion and 14 percent end in miscarriages.

which is not true for everyone. The health-related issues of teen pregnancy are also tied to many social factors, such as age, race, and socioeconomic status, all of which may affect the health outcome of a teen pregnancy. For this reason, not only does teen pregnancy have a place in national debates over public health, but it has become highly contested as a social problem in the United States as well.

SOCIAL FACTORS THAT CONTRIBUTE TO TEEN PREGNANCY

As the debate continues over whether teen pregnancy is a public health problem in the United States, there is equal controversy over whether it also constitutes a social problem, which is an issue that threatens the prosperity or social well-being of a significant number of people. To be considered a social problem, an issue must be something that most people feel should be changed because it causes concern or fear for society and for the future. It is also something that people must believe can be fixed if society works together toward a solution. A social problem creates a gap between an ideal social situation and the situation that actually exists. Whether teen pregnancy is a social problem that truly threatens the well-being of society or whether it is only perceived as one has long been a matter of debate.

There is widespread belief that teen pregnancy is a significant social problem in the United States. Seemingly alarming statistics about teenagers getting pregnant and having babies have been at the forefront of the news media for decades, giving the impression that teen pregnancy is a prevalent and troubling issue. Teen pregnancy is reported as something that happens often all across America, with many negative consequences both for the teens who are directly affected and, indirectly, for society, which often must support teenage parents financially. Some people have gone so far as to compare teen pregnancy to a social plague of crisis proportions. "From an epidemic perspective," says Lisa Arai, "teenage pregnancy is a kind of blight with a viral-like nature, one that is . . . capable of spreading itself through a youthful population and able to withstand efforts to defeat it." She says that to people who have come to think of teen pregnancy as a dire social problem, "it is as if pregnant and parenting teenagers represent all the bad things in society."[41]

Why Pregnant Teens Are Called a Social Problem

The reasons for considering teen pregnancy to be a social problem are often linked to money. Teenage parents, and especially teenage mothers, are generally considered to face steeper economic challenges in life than their peers who put off parenthood, in part because waiting to have children makes it easier for a young woman to attend college or at least finish high school so she can find a job that pays well. Getting pregnant as a teen, especially for those who choose to give birth and keep their babies, significantly lowers the chances that a young woman will pursue higher education in her lifetime. Although the Guttmacher Institute says that increasing numbers of pregnant teens and teen mothers are obtaining high school diplomas through General Educational Development programs, about two-thirds of teens who become pregnant never finish high school, compared with only one-fifth of the general population. Also according to the Guttmacher Institute, only 1.5 percent of teen mothers receive a college degree by the time they are thirty, compared with about 28 percent of the total population.

Bearing and raising children too early in life can make it harder to get a high-paying job to provide for a family because better-paying and stable jobs, especially those with health care benefits for employees and their families, usually go to better-educated adults. People with a bachelor's degree typically earn almost twice as much as those who never graduated from high school and about 50 percent more than those who have no college degree. Likewise, much of society views these teens who put childbearing before education as problematic because they make life more difficult for themselves and often

Though an increasing number of girls obtain high school diplomas through GED programs about 66 percent of pregnant teens never finish high school.

rely on welfare. Teen mothers also have much higher odds of being on welfare at some point in their lives than women who wait until adulthood to have children. About half of all teen mothers go on welfare within five years of having their first child, and eight in ten teen mothers will rely on welfare at some point. These young mothers reflect the gap between what is usually perceived as an ideal situation—people becoming educated and having good jobs before starting families—and what often takes place across America—teenagers having children before they can provide for them.

The Teen Pregnancy Problem May Be Overstated

Teen pregnancy may not be quite the drastic and rampant social problem that some make it out to be, however. Despite a slight rise of about 3 percent in the teen pregnancy rate between 2005 and 2006, the teen pregnancy rate in the United States has significantly declined overall from what it was in the 1980s and early 1990s. This indicates that it is not a problem that is growing uncontrollably. The issue may be exaggerated for political reasons—teen pregnancy has become a popular topic that helps politicians take a public stand on social values like family and marriage. "It is partially a 'socially constructed' problem," say public policy researchers Alan Cribb and Peter Duncan. "Teenage pregnancy symbolizes broader concerns and anxieties about the nature and direction of modern society,"[42] things like the perception of declining family values. Despite often being described as a modern concern or one that has gotten worse in recent years, some researchers say that, like many public issues, teen pregnancy just falls in and out of popularity as a prevalent social problem, going through periods of intense study and then transforming into something the public ignores. If teen pregnancy is in a period of analysis from the public, however, the attention to it has been intense for years as magazines, newspapers, and daily television news programs consistently keep the issue in front of the public.

Teenagers, Sex, Pregnancy, and the Media

The belief that teen pregnancy has become a social problem of epidemic proportions is often circulated by the news media, which frequently report on teen pregnancy trends and may give the American public—particularly American adults, who are the largest audience for news media—the idea that teen pregnancy is both a prevalent social problem and a dangerous one for America's teens. "Most people's perceptions of pregnant and parenting teenagers derive *entirely* from media sources,"[43] says Arai. However, statistics about teenagers who are pregnant may be misunderstood or exaggerated, perhaps to the point of portraying the issue as a major social problem when it may not be one. "Journalists covering teenage pregnancy and, through them, their readers, often fail to understand the implications of the [statistics] they are presented with and will readily accept their validity without proper consideration,"[44] says Arai. The teen pregnancy rates reported in the U.S. media are generally factual, but if the news media portray the number of teen pregnancies as shocking and troubling news, public opinion about teen pregnancy may be swayed. As a result, say educational psychologists Sharon Lynn Nichols and Thomas L. Good, "the public, whose primary information about all youth sex comes from media accounts of pregnancy or abortion rates, erroneously believes that youth are hormonally driven sexual beings with little self control or responsibility."[45]

SEX SHOULD GIVE TEENS PAUSE

"In spite of genuine value conflicts among members of communities, it is both possible and crucial to continue encouraging the kind of social conservatism that gives young people pause for thought before becoming sexually active or having sex without protection."—Naomi Farber, professor of social work, University of South Carolina, Columbia.

Naomi Farber, *Adolescent Pregnancy: Policy and Prevention Services.* New York: Springer, 2009, p. 222.

For example, when the media report a teen pregnancy rate of 750,000 young women every year, the numbers sound shocking. Viewers and readers often conclude that rampant teen promiscuity must be behind such a large number of pregnant teens. The media rarely mention the opposing statistic: More than 90 percent of teenage girls in the United States avoid pregnancy each year. Nichols and Good also point out that media statistics of any kind are often misleading: "Statistics tell relatively little about the complicated nature of youth's sexual lives, and although they are useful indicators for gauging youth's sexual activity, they fail to provide accurate accounts of the conditions under which sexual behavior occurs."[46] For instance, Nichols and Good say that adults often see teen pregnancy rates as proof of oversexed teenage boys and girls; however, in more than half of pregnancies that occur among teens, the father is several years older than the teen mother, often not still a teenager himself. When sexuality between teenage girls and adult men is considered, say Nichols and Good, "we see a strikingly different picture from the common notion that young teens are irresponsibly following hormonal desires with each other."[47] This suggests that there may be much more behind the culture of American teenagers and their sexual practices than media statistics can show.

Some people believe that the media are also partly responsible for promoting teenage sexuality that leads to pregnancy, not just for reporting teen pregnancy trends. "Our vast media culture is replete with explicit and implicit messages about youth sex and its role," say Nichols and Good. "Entertainment and advertising saturate the market with sexual content and images of youthful, physical beauty. According to these messages, sex is exciting, healthy, and a powerful determiner of individual worth."[48] It may not be surprising, with the media onslaught of sexual content in the past few decades, that more teenagers might be experimenting with sex. According to pediatric health researcher Rebecca Collins and her colleagues, "TV may create the illusion that sex is more central to daily life than it truly is and may promote sexual initiation as a result. Teens who see characters having casual sex without experiencing negative consequences will be more likely to adopt the behaviors portrayed."[49] Nichols and

Voices for Abstinence

Sex in the media is often blamed for having a role in teen pregnancy, and songs with racy lyrics and even racier music videos have especially been accused of idolizing sexuality and making casual sex seem tempting to teens. Pop singer Lady Gaga is one star who has achieved notoriety by making music videos and stage appearances while scantily dressed and singing about sexually suggestive topics. Yet Lady Gaga has become an outspoken supporter of abstinence, which seems to have become a trend among many teenage stars as well. Miley Cyrus, Selena Gomez, and Jordin Sparks have pub-licly supported abstinence, and all of the Jonas Brothers took virginity pledges in their teens. Not all famous teens choose to promote abstinence, however. For example, Jamie Lynn Spears, television star of the Nickelodeon sitcom *Zoey 101* and younger sister of singer Britney Spears, became pregnant at age sixteen, to the dismay of many parents of young girls who had considered Spears's title character, Zoey Brooks, a wholesome role model for girls. The verdict is still out, however, on whether the media actually contributes to teen pregnancy, and stars may have less influence—good or bad—than they or the public believe.

Pop singer Lady Gaga has made her reputation from being scantily dressed and sexually suggestive on stage but has been an outspoken supporter of teen abstinence.

Good, however, contend that the media should not necessarily be assumed to be a bad influence on teens and that "there is some evidence that sex in the media helps youth make decisions and sort out complex sexual situations."[50] Seeing teenagers in movies and television programs who are faced with sexual decisions could help real-life teenagers decide what their own beliefs and attitudes are about sex and its consequences.

Teen Pregnancy, Race, and Culture

Whatever effects the media may have on the public perception of teen pregnancy as a problem, one of the most reported aspects of teen pregnancy has to do with its ties to race. Statistically, females in certain minority groups are more likely than women of other groups to become pregnant before age twenty, and teens who are African American or Hispanic have the highest teen pregnancy rate of all ethnicities in the United States. According to the Guttmacher Institute, approximately 12 percent of African American and Hispanic teens ages fifteen to nineteen become pregnant in the United States each year. This is three times higher than the percentage of white teenagers the same age who become pregnant every year, about 4 percent. Teenage girls who are Native American have slightly lower rates of pregnancy than African Americans and Hispanics but still far higher than the teen pregnancy rate among whites. Such disparities are sometimes interpreted as evidence of persistent racial inequity in the United States. "Teenage and out-of-wedlock pregnancy has become a widely racialized issue," says social history professor Linda Gordon, an issue that is affected by "accelerating impoverishment and inequality."[51]

Another point of view, however, is that African American, Hispanic, and Native American cultures perhaps have different values about family, sexuality, and parenting than white culture does, and this should not necessarily be labeled by the media or by American society as a social problem. For example, Hispanic families sometimes celebrate a young woman's fifteenth birthday with a festival called a *quinceañera* because this is the age at which many Hispanic cultures have traditionally considered girls to become women who are ready to marry and start

In the United States approximately 12 percent of black and Hispanic teens become pregnant each year, nearly triple the rate of white teens.

families. "In Mexico and other Latin American countries, the Quinceañera once signaled that a girl was officially on the marriage market," states an article in the *New York Times*, and "as a result, some have viewed the Quinceañera as a sexual coming-of-age moment for girls."[52] Among many Hispanic Americans, the cultural tradition of the *quinceañera* continues, and it is possible that young Hispanic women generally think of themselves as adults at fifteen years old. Sexual relationships, even motherhood, among teens might not seem as taboo in the Hispanic culture as they are made out to be in mainstream American society.

A LOT TO ASK OF TEENS

"With the age of puberty decreasing and the age of first marriage increasing, the average American now spends some ten years being sexually mature and unmarried. . . . There's never been a generation in human history from whom this many years of abstinence-until-marriage has been expected."—Marty Klein, marriage, family, and sex therapist.

Marty Klein, *America's War on Sex: The Attack on Law, Lust, and Liberty.* Westport, CT: Praeger, 2006, p. 8.

Many teens in racial minority groups, especially teens who themselves were born to teenage mothers, may also have cultural attitudes that accept or even embrace the idea of parenthood in one's teens. "Early motherhood . . . within some cultures and ethnic groups is more of a social norm in comparison with the 'expected' age of motherhood within the general population,"[53] says sexual health researcher Rebecca French. The difference in teen pregnancy rates among various ethnicities in the United States is itself a complicated issue with many possible contributing causes, and it is not necessarily something that can simply be labeled an example of racial inequality. Suggesting that teen pregnancy rates among all minority cultures should be lowered to match the rate among whites might actually increase racial unfairness by implying that everyone in America should conform to standards set by the white culture.

Teen pregnancy certainly is not limited to cultural minorities in the United States, either. White teenagers may have the lowest rate of pregnancy per every one thousand teenage women, but this does not mean that teen pregnancy is not an issue among whites. White teens represent the largest actual number of teen pregnancies that occur in the United States each year. According to the Guttmacher Institute, about 277,000 white teens became pregnant in 2005, the most recent year for which the institute has collected data. This was higher than the number of African American or Hispanic teens who became pregnant that year (about 206,000 African American teens and about 209,000 Hispanic teens). Because teen pregnancy affects white as well as minority teenagers, some argue that it may not be a racial issue at all. Teen pregnancy "is an issue across all cultures, across all populations, and, to be frank, it has been a problem forever," says Martha Kello, an associate professor of child development. "Now, whether or not it is a racial culture that's the issue or whether or not it is one of economics, religion or education, that happens to be a major question."[54]

Pregnancy and Religion

As Kello points out, religion is another cultural factor that has become a significant part of the debate over teen pregnancy. Some people claim that teen pregnancy is a symptom of a society in which religion has become less important; they believe that stricter and more traditional religious values across society could actually reduce teen pregnancy. "The level of a young person's religious commitment almost always makes a difference to his/her sexual attitudes and practice," says Steven Emery-Wright, a Methodist minister and college lecturer. "Young people's faith will also most likely mirror that of their parents. An obvious consequence of this is that children of parents with strong Christian commitments will have a lower incidence of teenage pregnancy."[55] Stronger religious beliefs throughout the population will not necessarily reduce teen pregnancy, however. Evidence suggests that strict religious beliefs may actually add to the teen pregnancy problem. According to a 2010 survey conducted by the Pew Forum on Religion and Public Life, in 2009 teen pregnancy rates surged

Teens pray at an all-youth worship service in Georgetown, Kentucky. Some evidence suggests that strict religious beliefs may add to the teenage pregnancy problem.

in states such as Mississippi, which were rated as having conservative Christian values. The rise in the number of teen pregnancies in states with highly religious populations suggests that teen pregnancy is not necessarily a result of weakened religious values. "While religion certainly *influences* the sexual decision making of adolescents," states sociologist Mark D. Regnerus, "it infrequently *motivates* the actions of religious youth. In other words, religious teens do not often make sexual decisions for religious reasons."[56] Religion, like race, may have a certain effect on teen pregnancy rates, but it is not the sole cause or the sole means of prevention. Pregnancy occurs in teens of all cultures and religious beliefs, so there clearly is more to the issue of whether teens become pregnant than just their race or the type or extent of their religious values.

Teen Pregnancy and Poverty

Some say the common cultural link between teenagers and pregnancy has nothing to do with race or religion but instead with money. Economics is perhaps the most highly contested factor in the debate over teen pregnancy as a problematic social issue. On an individual level, poverty and teen pregnancy often occur together in the same populations. Communities that are economically poor tend to have much higher rates of teen pregnancy than do wealthier areas, regardless of the racial, ethnic, or religious makeup of those communities. On a wider scale, teen pregnancy is also related to the economic well-being of the country as a whole because the cost of providing for teen mothers and their babies sometimes falls on taxpayer-funded welfare programs. The U.S. government spends an estimated $7 billion or more every year to provide cash assistance to teenagers who become parents to help them pay for living expenses like housing and food. This money has become one of the most prominent aspects of the argument as to whether teen pregnancy is a social problem. "Many stereotypes have emerged about 'welfare moms,'" says cultural anthropologist Barbara Miller. "These women, some people believe, have babies *because* they want welfare money."[57] Because a majority of teens who become pregnant are already poor and may see few other economic prospects for their lives, there is concern that the promise of welfare benefits for unwed teen mothers may actually be an incentive for some teens to become pregnant.

Living in poverty is a strong predictor that a young woman will become pregnant before she is twenty, although not necessarily because she wants to qualify for welfare. It is estimated that about 60 percent of pregnant teenagers live in poverty when they become pregnant, and about 80 percent of those who give birth and become mothers will live in poverty and require welfare services at some point. Motherhood creates many challenges for a teen, making it less likely that she will ever graduate from high school, for example (less than half of teen mothers do), or will attend any kind of postsecondary school (only about 2 percent ever earn a college degree). Lacking these credentials, a teen mother is less likely than better-educated peers to find a job that pays her enough money to support her family without living in poverty and receiving welfare assistance. "Adolescent girls who become mothers have fewer options for their future," say Andrew L. Cherry, Mary E. Dillon, and Douglas Rugh. "Early childbearing often limits school and job possibilities for these girls, which helps explain why so many of the world's young mothers live in poverty."[58] With or without welfare, pregnancy is often considered an economic trap for teenagers; once they become parents, they may always struggle economically. "[Teen pregnancy] is the single most reliable predictor of welfare dependency in this country,"[59] says environmental health professor John B. Conway.

Statistically dooming pregnant teens to a life of poverty may not accurately describe the connection between youth pregnancy and being poor, however. In fact, much debate centers on whether poverty contributes to teen pregnancy or whether teen pregnancy causes poverty. "With disadvantage creating disadvantage," states educational psychologist Frank D. Cox, "it is no wonder that teen pregnancy is widely perceived as the very hub of the U.S. poverty cycle."[60] Yet those who advocate eliminating poverty as a way to reduce teen pregnancy in America may be giving poverty too large a role as a cause of teen pregnancy in the first place. "Poverty does not inevitably lead to unwed adolescents' pregnancies," says psychoanalyst Anne L. Dean. "Further, the eradication of poverty, if this were possible, would not speedily eliminate the unwed teenage pregnancy behavior pattern."[61] Even characterizing teen pregnancy as a social problem with ties to poverty might be doing a disservice to pregnant teenagers. "It seems that, at best, teenage pregnancy is something which young women 'drift into' because of otherwise unfulfilled and problematic lives," say Cribb and Duncan. "Does this mean that it cannot be seen as a positive choice, as an expression of personal autonomy, as a valid means of becoming fulfilled rather than simply as a barrier to fulfillment?"[62]

Many researchers say that classifying teen pregnancy as a social problem is unlikely to be helpful. Instead, they recommend that the focus be shifted from labeling teen pregnancy as a problem to finding effective ways for teens to learn about

The U.S. government spends $7 billion every year to provide cash assistance to teenage parents that helps pay for living expenses and food.

Pregnancy on the Big Screen

A movie called *Juno*, released in 2007, told the story of a fictional sixteen-year-old who got pregnant and gave her baby up for adoption. The film was touted as a romantic comedy and had a happy ending. It was nominated for four Oscars, but it was also widely criticized for giving an unrealistic picture of the consequences of teen pregnancy because Juno's baby was adopted, and the teen moved on with life as if little had changed. In reality, though, only 2 percent of teen mothers actually give their babies up for adoption. The movie also was criticized because Juno came from a supportive family when a majority of pregnant teen-

agers statistically have underprivileged lifestyles and do not feel supported emotionally or financially at home. *Juno* was accused of romanticizing teen pregnancy and showing it as quirky and not terribly serious. The movie's screenwriter, Diablo Cody, said she was not trying to write a movie about teen pregnancy but rather one about relationships. The movie was not necessarily meant to be factual or realistic, nor was it intended to teach a teen audience right from wrong. Nevertheless, the controversy surrounding *Juno* reflected the varied opinions about teen pregnancy, pregnant teens, and how the media depict them.

The 2007 movie about teen pregnancy, Juno, *spawned controversies that reflected society's varied opinions about teens and pregnancy.*

sexuality and its consequences. In this regard, adult bantering about teen pregnancy and its problem status may leave teens with little actual guidance on sexuality and parenthood. Amidst the controversy about how much of a health or social problem teen pregnancy is and how it should be addressed, American teens have been placed at the center of another great battle over teen pregnancy—how best to help the country's teens avoid pregnancy, or at least unintended pregnancy, in the first place.

CHAPTER 4

HOW CAN TEEN PREGNANCY BE REDUCED?

Although debate continues across the United States as to whether teen pregnancy constitutes a serious problem in terms of public health and society's well-being, few would say that no effort should be made to reduce teen pregnancy rates. Pregnant teenagers may or may not have more serious health risks than pregnant women who are older, but they certainly have added health risks over other teens who do not become pregnant. Teens who choose to give birth and raise their children also face more challenges socially, financially, and in terms of educational opportunities than teens who do not have children to look after. "The vast majority of babies born to single teens remain at home with their young mothers," say social work professors Charles Zastrow and Karen K. Kirst-Ashman. "This places these young women in a very different situation than their peers. . . . The additional responsibility of motherhood poses serious restrictions on the amount of time available"[63] for typical teen pastimes like socializing, going to school, and making career choices. Pregnant and parenting teens, then, could be seen as a disadvantaged group compared with nonpregnant or nonparenting peers.

Not all teen mothers will have health problems, live in poverty, or rely on welfare services. Many complete high school, and some even attend college. Thus, teen pregnancy does not by itself doom a young woman to an unsuccessful, poor, or unhappy life. Pregnancy does, however, lead to a number of social, physical, and financial hardships for many teens. For these reasons, many Americans—adults and teens combined—believe that teens should put off pregnancy and childbearing until their adult years. Many people believe it is society's responsibility to help teenagers prevent pregnancy that can lead to such disadvantages.

Yet even within this widely held belief that teen pregnancy carries negative consequences and that teenagers should be taught to prevent it, some disagreement exists. The age at

The age at which a teenager should be considered capable and responsible enough to raise a child is a matter of much debate.

which a teenager is or should be considered an adult responsible enough for parenthood is itself a matter of debate. For
example, two-thirds of all teenage pregnancies occur among
women who are eighteen or nineteen years old; by this age,
they are considered legal adults who can lawfully marry. Some
people question whether pregnancies among eighteen- and
nineteen-year-olds even belong in the same class of debate as
pregnancies among teens who are seventeen, sixteen, or younger, particularly if a pregnant eighteen-year-old is married or in
a committed relationship and intended to have a child. "We've
redefined adolescence as an extension of childhood," says sociologist Karen Sternheimer, "whereas it used to be a precursor to adulthood."[64] American society, which considers those
age eighteen or older to be mature enough to vote in elections
and join the military, is perhaps doing them a disservice to assume they are not mature enough to raise a child or to try to
teach them that this is the case. "We like to infantilize teens,
or focus on their bad behavior, even though some of them are
functioning as adults,"[65] Sternheimer explains. A public campaign against teen pregnancy may be unjust to many teenagers,
especially those older than eighteen who would choose to have
a child.

NOT AN EDUCATION

"The only thing my mother told me about sex is not to have it.
That's not really an education."—Jessica, age seventeen.

Quoted in National Campaign to Prevent Teen and Unplanned Pregnancy, *Parent Power:
What Parents Need to Know and Do to Help Prevent Teen Pregnancy*. Washington, DC:
National Campaign to Prevent Teen and Unplanned Pregnancy, p. 16. www.thenational
campaign.org/resources/pdf/pubs/ParentPwr.pdf.

The issue of whether, and at what age, teen pregnancy
should be prevented has largely become a matter of debate
over social values. Many people, teens included, believe that
the teen years, at least prior to high school graduation, are
simply too early for any young adult to become a parent. "I've

seen pregnant girls walking around the hall [at school]," a fifteen-year-old boy named Ted told CBS news. "It's overwhelming."[66] Other people say that the real argument is not about teen pregnancy but instead about whether teen parents are married and whether unwed pregnancies at any age are appropriate. "What we have called our 'teen pregnancy' crisis is not really about teenagers," says Maggie Gallagher, president of the Institute for Marriage and Public Policy, "nor is it really about pregnancy. . . . What has changed most in recent decades is not who gets pregnant, but who gets married."[67] Still other people avoid the controversial topic of marriage altogether and say that American society should focus on preventing unintended pregnancy among all women, especially teenagers. "The consequences of unintended pregnancy are not confined to those occurring in teenagers or unmarried couples," says the U.S. Department of Health and Human Services, but "for teenagers, the problems associated with unintended pregnancy are compounded. . . . Reducing unintended pregnancies is possible and necessary."[68] Yet even if the goal of preventing teen pregnancy is repositioned as cutting down on the number of unwanted pregnancies among teens, rather than negatively judging teen pregnancy in general, there is still a huge debate among adults and teens alike about the best way to reach that goal.

Abstinence for Pregnancy Prevention

Abstinence is the act of avoiding a certain activity as a means of also avoiding negative consequences associated with that activity. In discussions about sex, abstinence means refraining from some or all types of sexual contact with another person. Because abstinence is the only absolute way to avoid pregnancy, many people tout abstinence as the best method of pregnancy prevention that American society can recommend to teenagers. Many teenagers are themselves supportive of abstinence as the one fail-proof way to avoid pregnancy until they are ready. "Abstinence is the only surefire way to avoid getting pregnant," says college student Lynne Collenback. "It has become a matter

of what I believe is right and wrong for myself."[69] Teen abstinence, say its supporters, has the added benefit of preventing
the spread of sexually transmitted diseases such as gonorrhea
and HIV/AIDS, and it also shifts teenagers' attention from sex
and its possible consequences, both physical and emotional, to
more potentially beneficial pastimes like school and extracurricular activities.

During the late 1990s and early 2000s, the administrations
of President Bill Clinton and President George W. Bush both
were proactive in supporting a national abstinence education
program for America's teens. The policy coincided with changes
in the sexual activity and pregnancy patterns of America's teens,
including a 10 percent drop from 1995 to 2002 in the number
of high school teenagers who had ever had sex and an approximately 36 percent drop in teen pregnancy rates during the same

Teens of the Pure Love Alliance march in Washington, D.C., in support of
abstinence.

period. "Programs will work that encourage our young people to abstain from at-risk sexual behavior,"[70] said Bruce Cook, spokesperson of a nonprofit group that supported abstinence-focused education, in 2001. To proponents of abstinence during the early 2000s, it seemed that more teenagers were remaining abstinent longer and that this was reducing teen pregnancy rates. "The more teens clearly understand the benefits to abstinence until marriage and the risks of premarital sexual behavior the more they will make the right choices,"[71] Cook said.

The idea of abstinence as a national policy for preventing teen pregnancy in the United States has been criticized, however, in part because those who support abstinence, especially abstinence until marriage, may make certain value judgments. For example, they may claim that premarital sex is immoral or that sexually active teenagers have made poor moral decisions. Not all Americans believe that marriage is or should be a goal for teenagers; therefore, a philosophy that puts marriage before sex simply does not make sense for some teens. A number of people, adults and teenagers alike, also believe the expectation that teenagers should remain abstinent until marriage or at least until adulthood is unrealistic and even counterproductive. They believe that abstinence programs set teenagers up to feel like they have not succeeded at an important expectation if they do have sex. "We are training a whole generation that 'if' (actually *when*) they have sex before marriage, that they have failed," says Marty Klein. "Over 90 percent of abstinence pledgers have intercourse before marriage—and they protect themselves and each other at a lower rate than nonpledgers."[72]

As Klein points out, those who are taught to practice abstinence and abstinence only are actually less likely to use a form of birth control, such as condoms, if they do have sex than are teenagers who are taught about alternatives to abstinence. This contributes to evidence that promoting abstinence as the only real way to prevent pregnancy could perhaps result in more teenagers engaging in unprotected sexual relationships that may result in pregnancy. Those who oppose abstinence-only education do not necessarily think the suggestion that "abstinence is best" encourages teenagers to rebel and have sex;

rather, they feel that it contributes to teen pregnancy by not giving teenagers information or alternatives to avoid pregnancy if they do have sex. "Kids don't abstain," says Klein. "The only question is whether they will have [sex] in a physically and emotionally healthy environment. . . . Abstinence programs assure they won't."[73]

There is no argument that abstinence is the only totally fail-proof method of preventing pregnancy—as long as those who practice it never slip up. "Abstinence is 100 percent safe," explain Margaret O. Hyde and Elizabeth H. Forsyth, authors of numerous books on health and social studies for young adults, but "this is true only when it is practiced 100 percent of the time."[74] Many people are skeptical that teenagers, as a population, will be committed to abstinence enough to practice it unfailingly. In fact, some teenagers never plan to remain abstinent, and even many who claim to believe strongly in abstinence become sexually active anyway. Therefore, teaching teenagers how to have sex safely may be preferable to setting up an unrealistic expectation for them not to have sex and then giving them no information about preventing pregnancy if they do become sexually active.

Teaching Safe Sex

Proponents of a comprehensive approach to teaching teens about sex state that, in order to really prevent pregnancy, teenagers need factual, scientific information about the sexual process. This approach, sometimes also called "abstinence-plus" education, promotes abstinence as only one of many options for preventing pregnancy before teenagers are ready to be parents. Rather than stopping at the message that abstinence is best, the comprehensive approach gives a broader view of pregnancy prevention. It discusses the various contraceptives, or birth control methods, that are available to teenagers, including prescription birth control pills, injections, and skin patches, all of which release pregnancy-preventing hormones into a woman's body. Most comprehensive sex education programs also teach the proper use of condoms, which are important not just to prevent pregnancy but also to reduce the risk of

School Rules for Pregnant Teenagers

Before 1972, public schools in the United States could prohibit pregnant teens from attending classes or participating in extracurricular activities based on the assumption that pregnancy made it impossible for a young woman to do well in school. It was also widely believed that a pregnant classmate would distract other students. In 1972 national legislation called Title IX was passed to eliminate gender-based discrimination in schools. In addition to giving young women the same opportunities men had to take certain classes, participate in sports, and attend college, Title IX made it illegal for U.S. public schools to treat pregnant students differently than any other students. Pregnant teenagers now have the right to attend school up to the day they give birth, to participate in all sports and extracurricular activities, and to be granted a period of excused absence from school once the baby is born. After Title IX was passed, the school dropout rate for pregnant teenagers declined by one-third. Today, many schools even provide special study programs, such as evening and correspondence classes, to make it easier for teenage mothers to complete their education and improve their opportunities for the future.

exchanging sexually transmitted infections and diseases such as chlamydia or HIV/AIDS. Many programs give teenagers information about the emotional aspects of sexual relationships as well, a topic not covered in abstinence-only programs. Most also provide birth control information for teenagers who are already sexually active and who are therefore neglected by programs whose main message is that they should have remained abstinent. Rather than keeping important information from teens, as abstinence-only programs are often accused of doing, supporters of a comprehensive sex education approach are in favor of giving teens access to information they need in order to make decisions about their own sexuality. "Abstinence-only programs are inherently coercive," say adolescent health physicians John Santelli and his colleagues, "withholding information needed to make informed choices and promoting questionable and inaccurate opinions."[75]

Supporters of comprehensive sex education claim it is more effective at reducing teen pregnancy than teaching only about abstinence. Proponents believe that if teenagers do become sexually active, they do so with knowledge about how pregnancy occurs and how to prevent it. Many teenagers say they appreciate programs that teach facts about sex objectively and scientifically, rather than programs that moralize and try to shape their sexual behavior or that do not give all the facts. "Teenagers are not all stupid, but all of us need help," says Bethany, age seventeen. "Don't hold back from 'the talk' or sharing information hoping that it will protect your children, because it only hurts when they get the wrong information."[76] According to a 2003 national survey of teenagers conducted by the Kaiser Family Foundation, a nonprofit organization that studies health care issues facing the United States, more than three-quarters of adolescents and young adults agreed that they need accurate information on sexual health topics, including how to properly use condoms. The survey was conducted during a widespread shift to abstinence-only education in the United States, and it indicated that teenagers wanted more information about safe sex, not just advice to avoid sex. "Young people," reported the Kaiser Family Foundation survey, "feel great pressure to have sex, with a majority saying that while putting off sex may be a 'nice idea, nobody really does.'"[77] Comprehensive sex education aims to give teenagers enough facts and information to make informed decisions about sex, despite whether they choose to become sexually active.

Supporters of a more conservative approach to sex education, meanwhile, argue that abstinence-plus education may actually give teenagers mixed messages about protecting themselves from pregnancy. Many opponents of comprehensive sex education say such programs teach that abstinence is best but then give detailed information about what to do if teenagers fail to remain abstinent. Abstinence-plus programs are sometimes blamed for giving teenagers the idea that it is okay, and even expected, that they will become sexually active before adulthood. "They [supporters of comprehensive sex education] want to sabotage the authentic abstinence message by including instruction in condom and contraception use," says Emma Elliott, writing for a conservative coalition called Concerned Women for America. "That's a mixed message. We don't tell children not to do drugs and then give them clean syringes in case they do. We don't tell them not to smoke and then give them low-tar cigarettes because those are

Most comprehensive sex education programs teach the proper use of condoms, which are important for preventing unwanted pregnancy and reducing the risk of exchanging sexually transmitted diseases (STDs).

the least harmful."[78] Many proponents of abstinence-only education fear that comprehensive sex education will lead teens to engage in sexual behavior that puts them at risk for becoming pregnant.

KNOWLEDGE IS POWER

"Give young people the tools and, more and more, they will make safe and responsible decisions. Deprive them of critical information, and we'll continue our dubious track record as the least successful nation in the western industrialized world in dealing with teens and sexuality."—James Wagoner, president of Advocates for Youth.

James Wagoner, "Teens Need Information, Not Censorship," National Coalition Against Censorship Press Event, June 12, 2001. www.advocatesforyouth.org/index.php?option=com_content&task=view&id=761&Itemid=58.

Whereas opponents of abstinence-only education say that teenagers are unlikely to be abstinent 100 percent of the time, opponents of comprehensive sex education similarly argue that birth control methods are highly effective only when used, and used correctly, 100 percent of the time. Sexually active teenagers are not this faithful to the use of birth control methods, says the National Campaign to Prevent Teen and Unplanned Pregnancy—as many as one-third of sexually active teenagers who use some form of birth control do so inconsistently. And although supporters of comprehensive sex education believe that this statistic merely means more should be taught to teenagers about the importance of consistently using birth control methods, people who favor abstinence-only education disagree, saying that any sex among teens is exposing them to unnecessary risk of pregnancy. The American College of Pediatricians, for example, states that it "strongly endorses abstinence-until-marriage sex education and recommends adoption by all school systems in lieu of 'comprehensive sex education.'" It says this position is "based on the public health principle of primary prevention—risk avoidance in lieu of risk reduction, upholding the 'human right to the highest attainable standard of health.'"[79] In other words, it may not be enough to merely lessen a teen's risk of pregnancy by improving access to and use of birth control. Abstinence proponents say society is obligated to try to eliminate the risk of unwanted pregnancy altogether, and that abstinence is the only completely effective way.

Proponents of comprehensive teen sex education support the use of birth control. Statistics show that the one-third of teenagers who do use birth control do so inconsistently.

Sex Education in the Cross Fire

Abstinence-only and abstinence-plus education supporters both face opposition, not just from people with different beliefs about the best way to teach America's teenagers about sex and the prevention of pregnancy but also from people who disagree about where—and whether—such lessons should even be taught. Public schools have become a battleground for the debate on sex education; the vast majority of America's teenagers attend public schools, so these have become the most obvious settings in which to give information to teens about sex and pregnancy. "The many public consequences of sexual activity among teenagers make [sex education] an appropriate subject for public education,"[80] says political writer Amy Gutmann. The intense controversy about which sexual information is best—such as abstinence or abstinence-plus— is sometimes compounded by communities that question not only which program to use but who should decide what gets taught. "Many different types of organizations now play an important role in sexuality education," say sex educators Clint Bruess and Jerrold Greenberg. "The schools have remained a basic potential source of sexuality education programs, but religious organizations, voluntary agencies, health departments, professional schools, and even clubs now contribute to overall sexuality education efforts."[81] Even if schools, school districts, parents, and other organizations can reach a consensus on the type of program that is best, such as abstinence or abstinence-plus, it is still difficult to narrow down the specific information that will be most useful and the best materials and methods for teaching it. "Today, the problem is often in wading through the many resources to evaluate them and decide which are most useful,"[82] say Bruess and Greenberg.

Adding to the controversy over what should be taught with regard to sex education, in many communities parents with differing opinions argue over whether it is a public school's place to teach children about sex. "Schools need to focus on academics and leave teaching about 'the rest of life' or 'personal life' to parents," argues conservative blogger Lisa H. Warren. "The govern-

The Morning-After Pill

A kind of medication known as emergency contraception is available for women to take after having unprotected sex in order to prevent an unwanted pregnancy. Commonly called the morning-after pill, this medication actually can be used up to five days after unprotected sex, although it is most effective if a woman takes it within one day. The medication is a dose of hormones, similar to birth control pills, that prevents the woman's body from releasing an egg and/or prevents a fertilized egg from embedding in the uterus. Although emergency contraception is not a failproof method (it only reduces the risk of pregnancy by about 80 percent), it could prevent unwanted pregnancy among teenagers who have had unprotected sex and regret it immediately afterward. Yet dispute over when life begins—at fertilization or when the egg embeds in the uterine wall—has led to much controversy over this birth control option because some people believe it may actually be killing an already conceived child. That, combined with the cost of the pill—anywhere from ten dollars to more than two hundred dollars per dose—and the necessity of getting the pill by prescription from a doctor, could make this an unrealistic option for many teenagers.

The high cost of the morning-after pill precludes its use by teens.

ment (public school) has no right to attempt to involve itself in matters of morality and sexuality."[83] At best, the sex education curriculum taught in many communities is closely monitored by parents who may challenge whether the content is appropriate. School districts, not wanting to create controversy among parents, sometimes find themselves forced to restrict or compromise on what they can teach teenagers about sexuality, safe sex, and prevention of teen pregnancy. "Mandatory sex education is as offensive to parents who believe in the sanctity of sex as mandatory prayer is to parents who do not believe in God," says Gutmann. At the same time, she says, "teenagers, not their parents, are required to take sex education courses."[84] Many teenagers, however, say they appreciate the opportunity to learn about things like pregnancy and its prevention in school. "Sexual education is a valuable topic," says Karen, a high school sophomore in Indiana. "If we didn't have that class, many of us would have unsafe sex, simply because we don't know how to use contraceptives."[85]

Whether as a means of discouraging sexual activity that leads to pregnancy among teens or of encouraging use of contraceptives and other safe-sex practices to reduce consequences such as pregnancy, sex education is likely to be an imperfect attempt to address unwanted teen pregnancies and their effects on teens and on society. Most Americans agree that teenagers need some sort of guidance from adults if they are to approach sexual situations maturely, responsibly, and in ways that do not lead to unwanted pregnancy. Yet harsh disagreements continue over whether and what lessons on sexuality should be taught in public schools. "It is a shame that adults and policymakers spend their time arguing over what is better and more effective: abstinence-only sex education or education about contraceptives," says teen activist Caitlin Shetter. "While they are arguing, thousands of teens are having sex and getting pregnant."[86]

Furthermore, while formal sex education remains in dispute, teenagers are constantly surrounded by depictions of sex. A primary source of this exposure is the media, and in the absence of consistent sex education in schools, television and movies could be where teens turn most often to learn about sexuality. About

About 70 percent of the most popular television shows among teens show sexual content. Studies show the amount of TV sexual content viewed directly affects promiscuity among teens.

70 percent of the most popular television shows among teenagers show sexual content, according to the Kaiser Family Foundation; and a 2004 study by the Rand Corporation showed that teens who watched the most television with sexual content were twice as likely to have sex within the following year as teens who watched the least. While arguments rage over the issue of sex education, those who may be hurt most are the teens left to obtain the majority of their knowledge of sex and pregnancy prevention from television. "It is inexcusably lazy to let Hollywood and prime-time television stand in for accurate information about sex,"[87] says schoolteacher Courtney E. Martin.

Sex and pregnancy remain constant realities for American teens, despite all the controversies over how best to help teens avoid making sexual decisions that lead to unintended outcomes. Sex education efforts mired in controversy have proven ineffective at preventing hundreds of thousands of unintended pregnancies among teenagers each year. When these teenagers discover they are pregnant, they face additional controversy over how they should ultimately choose to respond to the situation.

TEENAGERS' OPTIONS FOR COPING WITH PREGNANCY

When a woman discovers she is pregnant, she may be happy, uncertain, or unhappy about the news. Her opinion depends on many factors, including whether she was actively trying to have a baby, whether she is in a committed relationship with someone who can help provide for the child, and whether she is physically, emotionally, and financially prepared to give birth to and raise a baby. Eighty percent of all teen pregnancies are unintentional, so pregnancy usually comes as a surprise to teens who discover they are expecting a baby. They suddenly are faced with complicated issues, such as whether or not to tell friends, family members, and the father of the child, for example. These decisions can weigh heavily on the minds of many newly pregnant teenagers, especially because American culture so often scorns teenage parents or stereotypes them as irresponsible and promiscuous. Although a pregnant young woman did not create the baby alone, she may be alone in facing scorn over the pregnancy because she—and not the father—is the one whose body will change. She is also the one whose future will be the most directly affected by the pregnancy and the decisions she makes about it.

Young women are faced with three choices when they learn about a pregnancy. All three choices have pros and cons, and none of them is without a certain amount of emotional turmoil and controversy. The woman can choose to end her pregnancy by getting an abortion. She can choose to carry the pregnancy to term, give birth to the baby, and then give the baby up for adoption. Or she can choose to give birth and raise the baby herself. Any of these decisions has consequences—physical, emotional,

A pregnant young girl is faced with one of three difficult choices. She can either end the pregnancy by abortion, carry the baby to term and give it up for adoption, or raise the baby herself.

and often financial—for a woman. Teenagers are usually more vulnerable to these consequences than older mothers because they live in a society where pregnancy at their age is a highly controversial issue with a negative stigma. Teenagers face extraordinary pressure and often very different messages from their peers, their families, and their communities about the best way to cope with pregnancy. A few, approximately 14 percent, will have a miscarriage—when a pregnancy ends spontaneously—but the rest will ultimately have to make one of the three choices.

Controversies over Abortion

Arguably the most controversial option available to pregnant teenagers has also become one of the most highly contested social issues in America today: abortion, a medical method by which a woman can end her pregnancy. Various abortion options are available. Prior to the tenth week of pregnancy, a woman can take medication that brings about a miscarriage (the loss of the developing baby). Abortion also can be performed by a surgical procedure that removes the embryo (what a developing baby is called in the first eight weeks of pregnancy) or the fetus (a developing baby nine or more weeks into pregnancy), along with the lining of the woman's uterus. Surgical abortions are usually performed during the first twelve weeks of a pregnancy. Most abortions are considered outpatient procedures, meaning that the patient does not need to be admitted to a hospital but can have the procedure in a doctor's office or clinic and go home the same day. Medically, an abortion is a fairly straightforward process. Although there is a small risk that a woman who has an abortion will have trouble getting pregnant again later in life or will have trouble carrying a later pregnancy for the full term, abortions are generally considered to have few if any long-term physical consequences. Compared with being pregnant for a full nine months and the physical toll that pregnancy and childbirth can take on a teen's body, abortion is sometimes even considered a preferable option for some pregnant teens, at least in terms of physical health. "Legal abortion, especially before 12 weeks, [is] over ten times safer physically than carrying a pregnancy to term," say Barbara M. Newman and Philip R. Newman, specialists in human development and family studies. Legal abortion, they say, is "one of the safest surgical procedures in the United States."[88]

For many teenagers abortion is an attractive choice for coping with an unplanned pregnancy because it also lessens or even eliminates the social stigma that a teen may feel or experience as a result of being pregnant. Many teens who discover they are pregnant feel embarrassed or ashamed and may wish to hide the pregnancy from their family, friends, or peers at school, to the extent that they may want to drop out of school, run away from home, or make other choices that could have long-term and negative effects on their lives. For some pregnant teens, abortion is a way to avoid the social stigma that goes along with pregnancy, and they may feel it is the best option available for them to complete their education and meet life goals. "I was just about to turn 19 and I was pregnant," says Tulalah, a college freshman who chose to have an abortion after learning she was pregnant. "I knew that I could not have the child. Not because I didn't want children, but I was not ready to take the responsibility for another life when I couldn't really provide for myself."[89]

ABANDONED MOTHERS

"I don't ever see [my son's] father. He's only a year older than I am and he wasn't ready to be a father. It was really hard for me to deal with having a baby without his support . . . but the responsibility is all my own. I'm a mother. I have to care for my child."—Renee, teenage mother.

Quoted in Margi Trapani, *Listen Up! Teenage Mothers Speak Out.* New York: Rosen, 2001, pp. 27–28.

Abortion is not without negative side effects, however. The process can be painful, causing severe cramping and also heavy bleeding from the woman's uterus. Complications, although rare, can include infection in the pelvis, blood clots, and damage to the reproductive organs. Abortions can also be physically dangerous if, in an effort to hide the pregnancy and abortion from everyone, a teenager opts to try to induce an abortion by herself, such as by ingesting dangerous substances to terminate her pregnancy. And because teenagers younger than eighteen are still minors, in thirty-four states they are unable to have an abortion without their parents' knowledge and/or consent, making abortion a difficult option for a teen who does not want her parents to know she is pregnant.

Abortion also is not without negative stigma. A woman who has an abortion may receive harsh treatment from other people if they know about the procedure because many Americans believe abortion is murder. Although a 1973 ruling by the U.S. Supreme Court, called *Roe v. Wade*, legalized abortion and gave

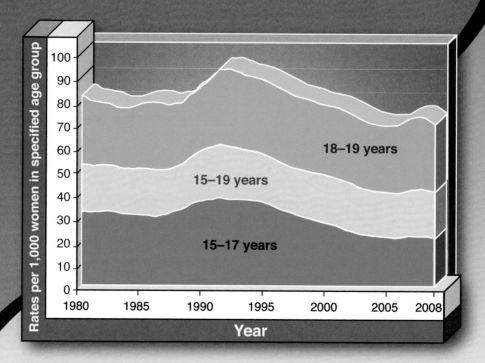

Teen Births in the United States, 1980–2008

Rates per 1,000 women in specified age group

18–19 years

15–19 years

15–17 years

Year

Taken from: CDC/NCHS. National Vital Statistics System. http://blog.thenationalcampaign.org/pregnant_pause/
TBR_graph_1980-2008.jpg.

all women in the United States the right to end an unwanted pregnancy, the decision has been attacked ever since by people who oppose abortion. "Usually a Supreme Court decision marks the end of a long legal struggle," says psychologist Simone Payment. "In the case of *Roe v. Wade*, another fight was about to begin. . . . Antiabortion groups quickly began organizing an attempt to overturn the Court's ruling."[90] Legal and social battles over *Roe v. Wade* have continued in the United States for decades. Because it is such an emotionally charged issue, women who choose abortion, even though they do so legally, may face a negative reaction from other people.

Due to the vast amount of social strife surrounding the abortion issue and the fact that many people—even some pregnant teenagers who have opted for abortion themselves—believe abortion is murder, having or even considering the procedure can cause intense feelings of guilt, shame, and regret. Some studies show that the abortion experience can take an emotional toll on a woman. In a society where the subject of abortion faces so much intense and sometimes fierce debate, teenagers who opt for abortion and are struggling emotionally with their decision may not feel they can talk about it openly before or after the fact. Abortion sometimes leads to depression, and feelings of sadness and regret can persist throughout a young woman's lifetime. "It hurts me that I killed my first child," says Marquisha, who had an abortion at age fifteen. "I hate to see baby things and pregnant people because it brings back memories."[91]

The link between abortion and depression is another area of dispute, however. One study, conducted by the University of Oregon and the University of California, San Francisco, in the early 2000s found that depression and low self-esteem were no more common among pregnant teenagers who chose abortion than among those who gave birth to their babies. Nevertheless, abortion is perhaps the most controversial of all the options a teenager has for dealing with an unplanned pregnancy, and many pregnant teenagers do not feel that abortion is right for them or that it is an accessible or practical choice. For these young women, continuing with a pregnancy and giving birth is the only other option. Their choices then come down to whether they will keep the baby or give him or her up for adoption after the birth.

Controversies over Adoption

Teens who learn they are pregnant tend to feel fear and uncertainty about the future. Few have been actively trying to become pregnant; most regard pregnancy as an accident or even a mistake. However, approximately 59 percent of all pregnant teenagers do not have a miscarriage and do not opt for abortion, according to the Guttmacher Institute. Despite the fact that the pregnancy may have been unexpected or even unwanted, they choose to remain pregnant and ultimately give birth. These expectant mothers often face difficult decisions about what to do during pregnancy and after the baby arrives. Most pregnant teenagers realize that delaying or quitting school will make life harder later on, yet continuing to go to class can be challenging for a pregnant teenager who is still in high school, for a number of reasons. The physical changes her body undergoes during pregnancy may make her tired and irritable, for example, and the changes to her appearance eventually become noticeable to other people, which can make her feel self-conscious or expose her to stares, gossip, and ridicule. She may even feel pressured by peers or by adults to drop out of school, at least during her pregnancy if not also afterward. And these pressures and difficulties may seem like merely a precursor to other difficulties once the baby arrives.

Although the 1973 U.S. Supreme Court decision in Roe v. Wade *gave women the right to an abortion, many people want to take away that right.*

Facing the challenges of life as a teenage parent, a life in which many freedoms vanish and responsibilities increase dramatically, some pregnant teenagers decide that giving the baby up for adoption after it is born is the best choice, both for them and their baby. Most who make this decision cite two reasons: They realize that raising a child will impede their own goals and hopes for the future, and they also realize that as a teenager, with or without the help of the baby's father, they can provide fewer advantages for the child than adoptive parents who are older and whose lives are more stable. "At age sixteen, the last thing on my mind was becoming pregnant and facing decisions like adoption," says Susan, a teenage mother who made the choice to let someone adopt her baby. "I knew right away that it would not have been possible for me to provide the home that a child deserves. And I was not willing to make it my parents' responsibility."[92]

Adoption is widely considered a good option for pregnant teenagers, especially those who know they cannot or do not want to raise a child but who are philosophically opposed to abortion. Expectant teenage parents who decide on adoption often say they have made a choice to put their baby's needs ahead of their own. Others are motivated both by their baby's needs and an evaluation of their own limitations and of how life would be if they kept and raised a baby. "I wasn't interested in spending my life on welfare (or raising my baby that way)," says Shana, a teenage mother who gave her baby up for adoption. "I felt my child deserved more than spending his or her life in daycare, while I worked full-time (or more) to make ends meet." For teenage parents like Shana, adoption is a positive solution to a difficult situation. As Shana explains, "The entire decision has brought me much joy and peace."[93]

On the other hand, adoption is not without its downside. Unlike pregnant teenagers who opt for abortion, a pregnant teen who plans to give her baby up for adoption still faces the possible physical and health challenges of pregnancy to which teenagers are more susceptible. These include high blood pressure and other pregnancy complications as well as the risks teen pregnancy may create for babies, such as prematurity or low

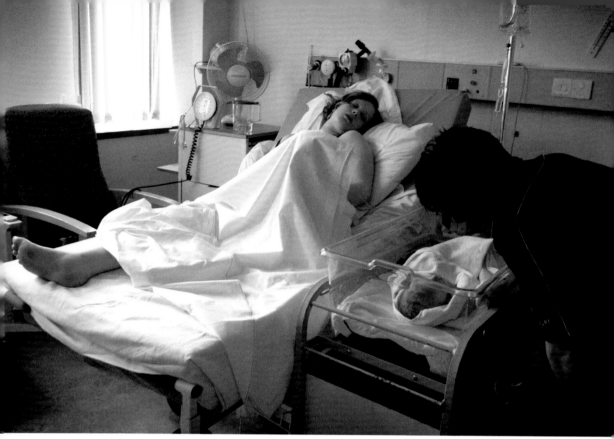

Many teenagers opt to give their baby up for adoption, though they must still face the rigors of childbirth, which may change their mind.

birth weight. Studies on adopted babies show they may have difficulty adjusting to adoptive parents. For example, adopted children have almost twice the risk of developing conditions like attention-deficit/hyperactivity disorder than do children who stay with their birth mother after they are born. Giving a child up for adoption may also have negative emotional effects on the teenage parents. Many teenage parents say that the decision to give their baby up for adoption is, at best, a heart-wrenching and extremely difficult decision, even if they believe they are doing the best thing for themselves and for their child. "The father and I knew we couldn't give our wonderful baby everything she needed or wanted," says Katharine, who at age sixteen gave a baby up for adoption. "It was the hardest thing we've ever done. Probably the hardest thing we'll ever do."[94] Some teenage parents who have given a child up for adoption even say they have lived with regret over that decision. "I did not do the 'loving thing' as much as I did the 'uninformed thing,'" says Laurie

Frisch, a woman in her forties who as a teenager agreed to have her daughter adopted. "I was led to believe that giving away a child would be more like giving away a puppy than actually losing your closest family member. And, I was told I would 'get over it.'. . . I never will."[95]

Adoption can also give teenage parents strong feelings of guilt or regret that may put them, especially mothers, at risk for depression both immediately after the adoption and in the years to come. "I am trying to get across to people . . . the lifelong effects that separation can have on the mother and the child,"[96] says Frisch. Although adoption is often considered an advantageous choice both for a teenage mother and her child, it is the least common choice pregnant teens make when deciding what to do about their pregnancy. In fact, only about 1 percent of teenage mothers choose to give their child up for adoption. "I sometimes wonder how [my daughter] would've turned out had she become another woman's child at one day of age,"[97] says Lois, who gave birth to a daughter at age fifteen and chose to be a single teenage mom. She raised her child to be a happy, healthy, college-bound young woman, a success story that shows that teenagers can make good parents. "I honestly don't know if I would've survived without [her] in my life all these years,"[98] Lois says about her daughter. It is a sentiment that most pregnant teenagers seem to share because very few make the choice to part with their child. The majority of teens who become pregnant in the United States give birth to and raise their babies.

Teenagers as Parents

Becoming a parent can be an exciting and positive event, no matter how old or young the parents are. Some studies have shown that approximately one in five of all teen pregnancies occur among young women who claim to want a child and who either intend to become pregnant or have said they would not be upset to learn they were pregnant. Some of these young women are in love with the father of their child; others simply want a baby. Even among the three-quarters of all teen pregnancies that are not intentional, the mother often chooses to keep her child. "They're so excited to finally have someone to

Teenage Fatherhood

Every child of a teenage mother has a father, too. Although it is common for the fathers to be several years older than the teenage mothers, many dads are still teenagers themselves. Society sometimes stereotypes teenage fathers as reckless, promiscuous, and unwilling to take responsibility for supporting their children. Teenage mothers are often portrayed as being left behind to raise a child while teenage fathers go on with life as usual. Yet research on teen dads has shown that these stereotypes are rarely true. A nationwide study in 2005 by New York City's Bank Street College of Education found that three-fourths of teenage fathers contributed financially to raising their child, and more than 80 percent saw their child almost every day. Teen fathers may even drop out of school in order to work full time to help with child expenses. Because education is so important to getting a good job that can support a family, providing teenage fathers with assistance and opportunities for staying in school could be one way to lessen the financial burden of parenthood for teenage mothers and fathers alike.

love them unconditionally,"[99] says Amanda Ireland, who had a baby during her freshman year of high school and says she was often approached by classmates who told her she was lucky to be a mom.

Unfortunately, not all stories of teen parents have happy endings. Teenage parenthood is often a tale of poverty and negative outcomes for both the parents and the children. Having a child is always a life-changing event and can be a considerable challenge for any parent, both financially and emotionally. For teenagers, the difficulties and stresses of parenthood are often made worse by their age. Depending on how old the mother and father are when the baby arrives, they still may be legal minors, which makes it difficult to obtain a place to live because they may not yet be legally able to rent. Some teenage parents are not even old enough to drive, or they may not be able to afford a car, gas and vehicle maintenance, car insurance, and other expenses related to driving. Without transportation, they may not be able to get to and from day care and work, making it difficult or impossible to keep a job, much less to complete a high school education. Many teenage parents depend on support from family members to make ends meet, to have a place to live, and to continue to pursue goals such as education. This often means that the new baby's other relatives, such as grandparents, aunts, and uncles, take on at least some of the financial and time burdens of raising

The difficulties and stresses of parenthood are often made worse when the mother is a teenager.

the baby. Although some teenage mothers do marry or live with the father of their child, many are single and often lack financial contributions from the father, who may claim he is not the one responsible for the child or who may not make enough money to help much with the costs of rearing the child.

BREAKING THE CYCLE

"My father was a parent when he was a teenager. My mother and grandmother were. It didn't stop with me or with my brothers. I know it will stop with my son."—Terry, teenage father.

Quoted in Richard Stengel, "Teenage Fathers: The Missing-Father Myth," *Time*, June 21, 2005. www.time.com/time/magazine/article/0,9171,1074862-2,00.html#xzz11OlxxTWD.

As desperate as the financial situation may be for many teenage parents and especially single teenage mothers, there are resources to help. Young mothers can apply for and receive welfare, which is funding from the government to help those in poverty pay for living expenses. There are also increasing resources for teenage mothers in many communities. Community health services often help provide basic but essential medical care for the child, such as immunizations and checkups, usually at a lower cost than private doctors. Child care is also provided in some public high schools to give young mothers the opportunity to obtain a high school diploma that will help them get a better job. These resources, however, are problematic for many Americans who believe that public services should not be available to teenage parents at taxpayers' cost and may even think teenage mothers are using such resources to avoid adult responsibility. "By the mid-1980s teen pregnancy had become linked with social welfare policy," says Wanda S. Pillow, a professor of education policy. "In this portrait of welfare dependency, the teen mother became the welfare dependent mother, the 'welfare queen.'"[100] For the past few decades, public opinion in America has not been favorable toward government-funded programs for teen mothers. During the welfare reform movement of the

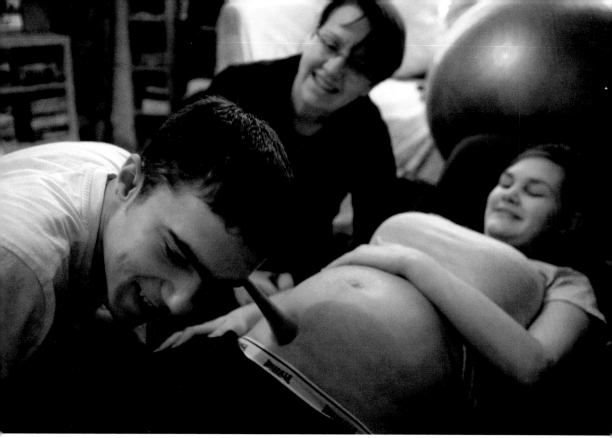

A nationwide study found that three-fourths of teenage fathers contributed financially to raising their child and over 80 percent saw their child almost every day.

1990s, a Kaiser Family Foundation poll showed that 64 percent of Americans felt the U.S. government was spending too much on welfare, and 56 percent believed the welfare system discouraged the formation of families by providing too many resources to unwed teen mothers. In 2010, according to *Public Opinion Monthly*, 71 percent of American voters said they believed government spending on everything was too high, and only 25 percent felt that the government should give more welfare money to poor families, including those headed by teenage mothers.

Perhaps because of such public views about welfare recipients, resources like welfare are not without drawbacks for teenage parents. If a young mother receives welfare benefits, they often come at their own cost to her. She is required to put her baby in a child care situation and work to supplement the welfare income as much as she can. Some young women also perceive a stigma attached to being on welfare or taking advantage of child care provided at a public high school where they

Homes for Pregnant Teens

Teenage girls living in poverty are the most likely of all teenagers to become pregnant, and pregnancy adds economic hardship to their lives, especially if they find themselves homeless. This is the case for many teens, such as those in foster homes (many of which will not house pregnant teens), those whose family has kicked them out because of the pregnancy, or those who were already homeless when they became pregnant. Group homes for pregnant teenagers and new teen mothers are a source of help. These government-funded facilities exist around the country and are safe places where teenagers can go to live during and after pregnancy. In return for shelter and food, teens who live in such homes are expected to make progress toward independence through work, school, classes on parenting and life skills, and household chores like cleaning, cooking, and grocery shopping. Such group homes often have strict rules, including curfews, early morning wake-up calls, and restrictions on visitors. Living there may not always be easy, but admission is competitive nonetheless because the homes give teens who are pregnant or are already mothers a temporary place to live and an opportunity to prepare for independent life.

may know other students and feel uncomfortable about being a mother at such a young age. And not all young parents pursue educational goals to try to secure a better future for themselves and their children. For many, pregnancy and parenthood at a young age do lead to a life of poverty and contribute to what has been identified as a poverty cycle: Girls who were born to teenage mothers are more likely to become mothers as teenagers themselves, and children born into poverty are more likely to remain in poverty once they are adults.

Still an Issue of Ongoing Debate

Teen pregnancy and the medical, social, and emotional costs created by young people having children before they are prepared to care for them are and will likely remain controversial issues in the United States. In the end, the most important debate may not be about the moral issues of whether or not teenagers are too promiscuous or whether teen pregnancy is really a serious health or social problem. It may not be about whether or what teenagers should be learning about sex in school, whether teenagers should choose not to keep their pregnancies or their babies, or how much financial help the government should give to those who do. The most important debate over teen pregnancy may come down to the best way to help young people make choices about their lives so that they do not have children before they are ready to take on the responsibility of raising them. If this goal is reached, teen pregnancy most likely will no longer be perceived as a threat to children and to society as a whole.

NOTES

Chapter 1: The Causes of Teen Pregnancy in America

1. Dave Bohon, "Survey Finds Americans Have Dim View of Nation's Moral Values," *New American*, May 31, 2010. www .thenewamerican.com/index.php/culture/family/3667-survey-finds-americans-have-dim-view-of-nations-moral-values.

2. Kerby Anderson, "The Teen Sexual Revolution," Leadership U, 2003. www.leaderU.com/orgs/probe/docs/sexrevol.html.

3. Quoted in *Good Morning America*, "Teens Speak Out on Palin's Pregnancy: GMA Hosts a Roundtable to Get Teens' Thoughts on Sex, Pregnancy," September 4, 2008. http:// abcnews.go.com/GMA/story?id=5725586&page=1.

4. Quoted in *Good Morning America,* "Teens Speak Out on Palin's Pregnancy."

5. Saul D. Hoffman and Rebecca A. Maynard, eds., *Kids Having Kids: Economic Costs and Social Consequences of Teen Pregnancy*, 2nd ed. Washington, DC: Urban Institute, 2008, p. 4.

6. Hoffman and Maynard, eds., *Kids Having Kids,* p. 4.

7. Quoted in Tara Parker-Pope, "The Myth of Rampant Teenage Promiscuity," *New York Times*, January 26, 2009, p. D6.

8. Family Connection of St. Joseph County, "Teenage Pregnancy," 1996. http://community.michiana.org/famconn/ teenpreg.html.

9. Alan Guttmacher Institute, *Can More Progress Be Made? Teenage Sexual and Reproductive Behaviors in Developed Countries.* Washington, DC: Alan Guttmacher Institute, 2001. www .guttmacher.org/pubs/eurosynth_rpt.pdf.

10. Quoted in Rob Stein, "Rise in Teenage Pregnancy Rate Spurs New Debate on Arresting It," *Washington Post*, January

26, 2010. www.washingtonpost.com/wp-dyn/content/art icle/2010/01/25/AR2010012503957.html.

11. Daniel Hart and Gustavo Carlo, "Moral Development in Adolescence," *Journal of Research on Adolescence*, vol. 15, no. 3, 2005, p. 224.

12. Andrew L. Cherry, Mary E. Dillon, and Douglas Rugh, eds., *Teenage Pregnancy: A Global View*. Westport, CT: Greenwood, 2001, pp. xii, xiv.

13. Guttmacher Institute, *Can More Progress Be Made?*, p. 69.

14. Family Connection of St. Joseph County, "Teenage Pregnancy."

15. Family Connection of St. Joseph County, "Teenage Pregnancy."

16. Frederica Mathewes-Green, "Let's Have More Teen Pregnancy," *National Review,* September 20, 2002. www.frederica .com/writings/lets-have-more-teen-pregnancy.html.

17. Cherry, Dillon, and Rugh, eds., *Teenage Pregnancy*, p. xv.

18. Guttmacher Institute, *Can More Progress Be Made?*, p. 4.

19. Marty Klein, *America's War on Sex: The Attack on Law, Lust, and Liberty*. Westport, CT: Praeger, 2006, p. 24.

20. Quoted in Sabrina Weill, *The Real Truth About Teens & Sex*. New York: Penguin, 2005, p. 104.

21. Guttmacher Institute, *Can More Progress Be Made?*, p. 2.

22. Nancy Gibbs, "Why Have Abortion Rates Fallen?" *Time*, January 12, 2008. www.time.com/time/nation/article/0,85 99,1705604,00.html.

23. Quoted in Gibbs, "Why Have Abortion Rates Fallen?"

24. Mathewes-Green, "Let's Have More Teen Pregnancy."

25. Family Connection of St. Joseph County, "Teenage Pregnancy."

26. Klein, *America's War on Sex*, p. 6.

Chapter 2: Is Teen Pregnancy a Public Health Problem?

27. Quoted in Lawrence S. Neinstein, ed., *Adolescent Health Care: A Practical Guide*, 5th ed. Philadelphia: Lippincott, Williams & Wilkins, 2008, p. 574.

28. Nancy T. Hatfield, *Broadribb's Introductory Pediatric Nursing*, 7th ed. Philadelphia: Lippincott, Williams & Wilkins, 2007, p. 618.

29. Eva M. Szigethy and Pedro Ruiz, "Depression Among Pregnant Adolescents: An Integrated Treatment Approach," *American Journal of Psychiatry*, vol. 158, no. 1, 2001, p. 24.

30. Jonathan D. Klein, "Adolescent Pregnancy: Current Trends and Issues," *Pediatrics*, vol. 116, no. 1, 2005, p. 285.

31. Stephen Maddocks, *United Nations Children's Fund Worldwatch Series*. Chicago: Raintree, 2004, p. 20.

32. Barbara Luke, *Every Pregnant Woman's Guide to Preventing Premature Birth*. Lincoln, NE: Authors Choice, 2002, pp. 4–5.

33. Jeffrey Roth et al., "The Risk of Teen Mothers Having Low Birth Weight Babies: Implications of Recent Medical Research for School Health Personnel," *Journal of School Health*, vol. 68, no. 7, 1998, pp. 272, 274.

34. Nweze Eunice Nnakwe, *Community Nutrition: Planning Health Promotion and Disease Prevention*. Sudbury, MA: Jones and Bartlett, 2009, p. 154.

35. Kathleen Sylvester, *Teenage Pregnancy: A Preventable Calamity*. Washington, DC: Progressive Policy Institute, 1994, pp. 1–2.

36. National Campaign to Prevent Teen and Unplanned Pregnancy, "Why It Matters: The Costs of Teen Childbearing." www.thenationalcampaign.org/why-it-matters/pdf/costs.pdf.

37. Janet Rich-Edwards, "Teen Pregnancy Is Not a Public Health Crisis in the United States. It Is Time We Made It One," *International Journal of Epidemiology*, vol. 31, 2002, p. 556.

38. Debbie A. Lawlor and Mary Shaw, "What a Difference a Year Makes: Too Little Too Late," *International Journal of Epidemiology*, vol. 31, 2002, p. 558.

39. Lisa Arai, *Teenage Pregnancy: The Making and Unmaking of a Problem*. Bristol, UK: Policy, 2009, p. 9.

40. Lawlor and Shaw, "What a Difference a Year Makes," p. 558.

Chapter 3: Social Factors That Contribute to Teen Pregnancy

41. Arai, *Teenage Pregnancy*, p. 48.

42. Alan Cribb and Peter Duncan, *Health Promotion and Professional Ethics*. Oxford, UK: Blackwell, 2002, p. 67.

43. Arai, *Teenage Pregnancy*, p. 39.

44. Arai, *Teenage Pregnancy*, pp. 39–40.

45. Sharon Lynn Nichols and Thomas L. Good, *America's Teenagers—Myths and Realities: Media Images, Schooling, and the Social Costs of Careless Indifference*. Mahwah, NJ: Lawrence Erlbaum, 2004, p. 92.

46. Nichols and Good, *America's Teenagers*, p. 96.

47. Nichols and Good, *America's Teenagers*, p. 96.

48. Nichols and Good, *America's Teenagers*, p. 84.

49. Rebecca L. Collins et al., "Watching Sex on Television Predicts Adolescent Initiation of Sexual Behavior," *Pediatrics*, vol. 114, 2004, p. e281. http://pediatrics.aappublications.org/cgi/reprint/114/3/e280.

50. Nichols and Good, *America's Teenagers*, p. 92.

51. Quoted in Allan M. Brandt and Paul Rozin, eds., *Morality and Health*. London: Routledge, 1997, p. 252.

52. *New York Times*, "In Hispanic Ritual, a Place for Faith and Celebration," January 5, 2008. www.nytimes.com/2008/01/05/us/05quin.html.

53. Quoted in Philip Baker et al., eds., *Teenage Pregnancy and Reproductive Health*. Dorchester, UK: Royal College of Obstetricians and Gynaecologists, 2007, p. 246.

54. Quoted in Lauren Wicks, "Breaking Down the Statistics: Teen Pregnancy Especially Prevalent Among African-Americans," *Suffolk (VA) News-Herald*, September 2, 2009. www.suffolknewsherald.com/news/2009/sep/02/breaking-down-statistics/.

55. Steven Emery-Wright, *Understanding Teenage Sexuality: A Foundation for Christian Relationships*. Singapore: Genesis, 2009, pp. 102–103.

56. Mark D. Regnerus, *Forbidden Fruit: Sex and Religion in the Lives of American Teenagers.* New York: Oxford University Press, 2007, p. 184.

57. Barbara Miller, *Teen Pregnancy and Poverty: The Economic Realities.* New York: Rosen, 1997, p. 31.

58. Cherry, Dillon, and Rugh, eds., *Teenage Pregnancy,* p. xii.

59. Quoted in Sana Loue and Beth E. Quill, eds., *Handbook of Rural Health.* New York: Kluwer Academic/Plenum, 2001, p. 41.

60. Frank D. Cox, *Human Intimacy: Marriage, the Family, and Its Meaning,* 10th ed. Belmont, CA: Wadsworth, 2009, p. 258.

61. Anne L. Dean, *Teenage Pregnancy: The Interaction of Psyche and Culture.* Hillsdale, NJ: Analytic, 1997, p. xiii.

62. Cribb and Duncan, *Health Promotion and Professional Ethics,* p. 72.

Chapter 4: How Can Teen Pregnancy Be Reduced?

63. Charles Zastrow and Karen K. Kirst-Ashman, *Understanding Human Behavior and the Social Environment,* 8th ed. Belmont, CA: Brooks/Cole, 2010, p. 267.

64. Quoted in Sarah Kershaw, "Now, the Bad News on Teenage Marriage," *New York Times,* September 4, 2008, p. G1.

65. Quoted in Kershaw, "Now, the Bad News on Teenage Marriage," p. G1.

66. Quoted in *CBS News New York Early Show,* "Is 12 Too Young to Start Dating? Kids Open Up About Dating and Sex," May 26, 2010. www.cbsnews.com/stories/2010/05/26/earlyshow/living/parenting/main6520486.shtml.

67. Maggie Gallagher, *The Age of Unwed Mothers: Is Teen Pregnancy the Problem? A Report to the Nation.* New York: Institute for American Values, 1999, p. 3.

68. U.S. Department of Health and Human Services, *Healthy People, 2010,* 2nd ed., vol. 1. Washington, DC: U.S. Government Printing Office, 2000, section 9, p. 5.

69. Lynne Collenback, "Why I Choose Abstinence," *San Angelo Abstinence Examiner,* June 4, 2010. www.examiner.com/x-

52012-San-Angelo-Abstinence-Examiner~y2010m6d4-
Why-I-Choose-Abstinence.

70. Quoted in Choosing the Best Publishing, "New Figures
Show Abstinence Emphasis Working," press release, April
10, 2001. www.choosingthebest.org/press_room/press_
release_1.htm.

71. Quoted in Choosing the Best Publishing, "New Figures
Show Abstinence Emphasis Working."

72. Klein, *America's War on Sex*, pp. 21–22.

73. Klein, *America's War on Sex*, p. 21.

74. Margaret O. Hyde and Elizabeth H. Forsyth, *Safe Sex 101:
An Overview for Teens*. Minneapolis: Twenty-First Century,
2006, pp. 63–64.

75. John Santelli et al., "Abstinence and Abstinence-Only Education: A Review of U.S. Policies and Programs," *Journal of
Adolescent Health*, vol. 38, 2006, p. 79.

76. Quoted in Sabrina Weill, *The Real Truth About Teens & Sex:
From Hooking Up to Friends with Benefits—What Teens Are
Thinking, Doing, and Talking About and How to Help Them
Make Smart Choices*. New York: Penguin, 2005, p. 21.

77. Kaiser Family Foundation, *National Survey of Adolescents and
Young Adults: Sexual Health Knowledge, Attitudes, and Experiences*. Menlo Park, CA: Kaiser Family Foundation, 2003,
p. 2. www.kff.org/youthhivstds/upload/National-Survey-of-
Adolescents-and-Young-Adults.pdf.

78. Emma Elliott, *What Your Teacher Didn't Tell You About Abstinence*. Washington, DC: Concerned Women for America,
2005. www.cwfa.org/brochures/cwa_abstinence_brochure
.pdf.

79. American College of Pediatricians, "Abstinence Education." www.americancollegeofpediatricians.org/Abstinence-
Education.html.

80. Amy Gutmann, *Democratic Education*. Princeton, NJ: Princeton University Press, 1987, p. 111.

81. Clint Bruess and Jerrold Greenberg, *Sexuality Education:
Theory and Practice*, 5th ed. Sudbury, MA: Jones and Bartlett,
2009, p. 31.

82. Bruess and Greenberg, *Sexuality Education*, p. 32.

83. Lisa H. Warren, "Understanding the Conservative Positions on Sex Education," Helium. www.helium.com/items/721779-understanding-the-conservative-positions-on-sex-education.

84. Gutmann, *Democratic Education*, p. 110.

85. Quoted in Family Education, "One Teen's Opinion: Why Sex Education Is Important," http://life.familyeducation.com/sex/teen/36177.html.

86. Quoted in Sylvia Magora, "Young Activists Passionate About Pregnancy Prevention," MTV News, Sex Etc. column, May 5, 2005. www.mtv.com/onair/ffyr/protect/sexetc_may_05.jhtml.

87. Courtney E. Martin, "Willful Ignorance," *American Prospect*, January 17, 2007. www.prospect.org/cs/articles?articleId=12382.

Chapter 5: Teenagers' Options for Coping with Pregnancy

88. Barbara M. Newman and Philip R. Newman, *Development Through Life: A Psychosocial Approach*, 10th ed. Belmont, CA: Wadsworth Cengage Learning, 2009, p. 125.

89. Quoted in Feminist Women's Health Center, "Tulalah's Story," February 2, 1999. www.fwhc.org/stories/tulalah.htm.

90. Simone Payment, *Supreme Court Cases Through Primary Sources:* Roe v. Wade, *the Right to Choose*. New York: Rosen, 2004, pp. 47–48.

91. Quoted at TeenBreaks.com, "Girls Who Aborted." www.teenbreaks.com/abortion/girlswhoaborted.cfm?start=35.

92. Quoted in Independent Adoption Center, "Susan's Story: I've Been Given a Chance to Pursue My Goals." www.adoptionhelp.org/birthmother/stories/susan.html.

93. Quoted in Independent Adoption Center, "Shana's Story: I Will Never Regret My Choice." www.adoptionhelp.org/birthmother/stories/shana.html.

94. Quoted in Independent Adoption Center, "Katharine's Story: I'm So Thankful for Open Adoption." www.adoptionhelp.org/birthmother/stories/katharine.html.

95. Laurie Frisch, "A Personal Adoption Story," A Mother's Song: Taking the Crisis out of Pregnancy, 2003. www.motherhelp.info/about_me.htm.

96. Frisch, "A Personal Adoption Story."

97. Quoted in A Mother's Song: Taking the Crisis out of Pregnancy, "Adoption or Teen Parenting?" www.motherhelp.info/adoption_letter.htm.

98. Quoted in A Mother's Song: Taking the Crisis out of Pregnancy, "Adoption or Teen Parenting?"

99. Quoted in Kathleen Kingsbury, "Pregnancy Boom at Gloucester High," *Time*, June 18, 2008. www.time.com/time/world/article/0,8599,1815845,00.html.

100. Wanda S. Pillow, *Unfit Subjects: Education Policy and the Teen Mother*. New York: RoutlegeFalmer, 2004, p. 33.

DISCUSSION QUESTIONS

Chapter 1: The Causes of Teen Pregnancy in America

1. What do you think causes teen pregnancy in the United States? Is it because American teenagers are promiscuous, because they prize children and family, or do you believe there is a different reason?

2. Do you agree that teenagers are incapable of coping maturely with sexual relationships and their consequences? Why or why not?

3. What, in your opinion, is the most likely reason why teen pregnancy rates are higher in the United States than in other developed countries?

Chapter 2: Is Teen Pregnancy a Public Health Problem?

1. What is your opinion about whether or not teen pregnancy is a public health problem? How would you support your answer?

2. The author describes several potential health risks, both for the mother and the baby, that are associated with teen pregnancy. Which risk do you think is the most serious and why?

3. Why do you think the health risks of pregnant teenagers are frequently cited by the media when health risks of pregnancy among women older than age forty are not?

Chapter 3: Social Factors That Contribute to Teen Pregnancy

1. Teen pregnancy rates are higher among Hispanics, African Americans, and Native Americans than among whites. Why

do you think this is the case? What might the United States do to correct the disparities?

2. Alan Cribb and Peter Duncan ask whether pregnancy might be a positive choice—an expression of personal autonomy or a means of becoming fulfilled—for teenagers. How would you answer this question?

3. What effect do you think a person's religious beliefs have on teen pregnancy?

Chapter 4: How Can Teen Pregnancy Be Reduced?

1. What are some advantages and disadvantages of abstinence-only and abstinence-plus education programs? Which do you think is more successful at preventing teen pregnancy and why?

2. What do you think teenagers need and want to learn in sex education programs?

3. How influential do you think sex education programs are on reducing teen pregnancy rates?

Chapter 5: Teenagers' Options for Coping with Pregnancy

1. The author writes that a pregnant teenager faces three choices: abortion, adoption, or keeping and raising the baby. Make an argument in favor of one choice over the others.

2. Teenage parents sometimes rely on welfare services to help raise their child. What limits or restrictions, if any, do you think should be placed on welfare recipients who are teenage parents? How much help should society give to teenagers who have children and choose to raise them?

3. The Supreme Court's decision in *Roe v. Wade* made abortion legal in the United States. What is your opinion about *Roe v. Wade*? How accessible do you think abortion should be to teens under age eighteen?

ORGANIZATIONS TO CONTACT

Advocates for Youth
2000 M St. NW, Suite 750
Washington, DC 20036
phone: (202) 419-3420
fax: (202) 419-1448
website: www.advocatesforyouth.org

This organization provides information and resources for teenagers, parents, teachers, and youth advocates on sex education, teen pregnancy, abortion, and childbearing, all from a perspective of youths' rights.

American College of Obstetricians and Gynecologists
PO Box 96920
Washington, DC 20090-6920
phone: (202) 638-5577
website: www.acog.org

The American College of Obstetricians and Gynecologists provides accurate information and the latest research about pregnancy and women's sexual health. The website has specific information and resources about teen pregnancy, informational booklets, and more.

American Pregnancy Association
1431 Greenway Dr., Suite 800
Irving, TX 75038
phone: (972) 550-0140
toll-free hotline: (866) 942-6466
fax: (972) 550-0800
e-mail: aph@thehelpline.org
website: www.americanpregnancy.org or www.thehelpline.org

This organization provides a national service geared toward teens and young adults to offer access to pregnancy information and support, including a free, confidential hotline.

Guttmacher Institute
1301 Connecticut Ave. NW, Suite 700
Washington, DC 20036
phone: (202) 296-4012
toll-free: (877) 823-0262
fax: (202) 223-5756
website: www.guttmacher.org

The aim of the Guttmacher Institute is to advance sexual and reproductive health worldwide through research and education. It is one of the U.S. government's leading providers of research and statistics on the nation's teen pregnancy trends.

Healthy Teen Network
1501 Saint Paul St., Suite 124
Baltimore, MD 21202
phone: (410) 685-0410
fax: (410) 685-0481
website: www.healthyteennetwork.org

The Healthy Teen Network is a national organization focused on adolescent health and well-being with emphasis on teen pregnancy prevention, pregnancy, and parenting.

National Campaign to Prevent Teen and Unplanned Pregnancy
1776 Massachusetts Ave. NW, Suite 200
Washington, DC 20036
phone: (202) 478-8500
fax: (202) 478-8588
website: www.thenationalcampaign.org

This organization provides education and resources to interested parties to help reduce the number of unintended pregnancies, especially among teenagers, in the United States each year.

Planned Parenthood Federation of America
434 W. Thirty-Third St.
New York, NY 10001

phone: (212) 541-7800
fax: (212) 245-1845
website: www.plannedparenthood.org

A leading sexual and reproductive health care provider and advocate in the United States, the Planned Parenthood Federation provides information and resources on birth control, pregnancy, relationships, and more.

FOR MORE INFORMATION

Books

Anrenee Englander, *Dear Diary, I'm Pregnant: Teenagers Talk About Pregnancy*. Rev. ed. Toronto, ON: Annick, 2010. Ten teenagers relate stories of their experiences with pregnancy, giving a personal perspective of real young women faced with this complicated issue.

Lisa Frick, *Current Controversies: Teenage Pregnancy and Parenting*. Detroit: Greenhaven, 2007. This book provides different arguments and viewpoints that society has about the issue of teen pregnancy and the many controversies surrounding it.

Jeanne Warren Lindsay, *Teen Dads: Rights, Responsibilities & Joys*. Buena Park, CA: Morning Glory, 2008. This book provides information, particularly for young men, on options surrounding teen pregnancy, family planning, and the experience of parenthood. It supplements the many books directed at teenage girls and their responsibilities for preventing pregnancy or dealing with one.

Periodicals

Ross Douthat, "Red Family, Blue Family," *New York Times*, May 9, 2010. Differences between Republican and Democratic beliefs about marriage and teen pregnancy are highlighted as well as how teen pregnancy has become a part of an ongoing political debate.

Molly Lopez, Jill Smolowe, and Michelle Saber, "Teen Pregnancy: Growing Up Too Fast," *People*, January 14, 2008. The article gives six first-person accounts from girls ages sixteen to nineteen who became pregnant and how they responded to the news.

Internet Sources

Belinda Luscombe, "New Data: Teen Pregnancy on the Rise, Abortions Too," *Time*, January 26, 2010. www.time.com/time/health/article/0,8599,1956645,00.html#ixzz0t8T182GL. This article discusses a small rise (3 percent) in teen pregnancy rates during the mid-2000s that teen pregnancy researchers and policy makers found disturbing. Links to additional articles about teen pregnancy provide different viewpoints.

Jessica Press, "The Secret Life of Pregnant Teenagers," *Seventeen*, June 2009. www.thenationalcampaign.org/media/PDF/2009/seventeen_June09.pdf. *Seventeen* magazine provides various statistics and viewpoints about the issue of teen pregnancy in a format that is reader friendly.

Websites

Advocates for Youth (www.advocatesforyouth.org). This site presents background information on teen pregnancy in the United States; articles about pregnancy, contraception, and reproductive health for teens; and links to scholarly research and studies on teen pregnancy.

Medline Plus (www.nlm.nih.gov/medlineplus/teenagepregnancy.html). Through the section "Teenage Pregnancy," Medline Plus, a service of the National Institutes of Health, offers accurate medical information about different aspects of teen pregnancy as well as links to helpful websites, journal articles, and more.

Pregnant Teen Help (www.pregnantteenhelp.org). This website provides information about teen pregnancy for both adults and teenagers, with sections on pregnancy prevention, abortion, adoption, and resources for teens who are pregnant.

Women's Health Channel (www.womenshealthchannel.com/teenpregnancy/index.shtml). In the section "Overview, Consequences of Teenage Pregnancy," this website discusses the health issues of pregnant teenagers, teen mothers, and their babies along with information on birth control, teen pregnancy resources, and personal accounts from pregnant teens.

INDEX

PICTURE CREDITS

Cover: © Image Source/Corbis
AJPhoto/Photo Researchers, Inc., 8
AP Images/Breck Smither, 54
AP Images/Daniel Hulshizer, 39
AP Images/J. Pat Carter, 51
AP Images/Lisa Poole, 18
AP Images/Stacie Freudenberg, 82
© B R Bratby/Alamy, 77
BSIP/Photo Researchers, Inc., 33
Burger/Phanie/Photo Researchers, Inc., 73
© Catchlight Visual Services/Alamy, 17
© Chris Rout/Alamy, 87
© David J. Green-Lifestyle/Alamy, 30
© David-Young Wolff/Alamy, 45
© Dennis MacDonald/Alamy, 71
Fox Searchlight/The Kobal Collection/Gregory, Doane, 58
Gale/Cengage, 11, 80
Ian Hooten/Photo Researchers, Inc., 23
© Janine Wiedel Photolibrary/Alamy, 36, 75
J.H. Saunders/Landov, 49
Jim Varney/Photo Researchers, Inc., 61
© Kelly Boreson/Shutterstock.com, 41
Matt Jones/The Washington Times/Landov, 64
© Monkey Business Images/Shutterstock.com, 15
Nick Vedros & Associates/Getty Images, 57
© Patrick Bloomfield/Alamy, 69
© Rob Bartee/Alamy, 27
Tina Stallard/Getty Images, 84, 89
Win McNamee/Getty Images, 13

ABOUT THE AUTHOR

Jenny MacKay is the author of ten nonfiction books for middle graders and teens. She has a master of fine arts degree in creative writing from National University and lives with her family in northern Nevada, where she was born and raised.